Day by day

LYNDA RICHARDSON

TEACHER
TIMESAVERS

Published by Scholastic Publications Ltd,
Villiers House,
Clarendon Avenue,
Leamington Spa,
Warwickshire CV32 5PR

© 1995 Scholastic Publications Ltd
Text © 1995 Phil Newton and Lynda Richardson

Authors Phil Newton and Lynda Richardson
Editor Jo Saxelby-Jennings
Assistant editor Joanne Boden
Series designer Joy White
Designer Tracey Ramsey
Illustrations Peter Dennis (Linda Rogers Associates)
Cover illustration Frances Lloyd
Cover photograph Martyn Chillmaid

Designed using Aldus Pagemaker
Printed in Great Britain by Clays Ltd, Bungay, Suffolk

British Library Cataloguing-in-Publication Data
A catalogue record for this book is
available from the British Library.

ISBN 0-590-53195-6

**The authors and publishers wish to thank the following
individuals and organisations for their help in the
preparation of this publication:**
page 38, stamp outlines reproduced courtesy
of Royal Mail;
page 51 and 68, Royal Mint;
page 55, Eurotunnel Exhibition Centre;
page 65, "Panda device © 1986 WWF – World Wide Fund
For Nature (formerly the World Wildlife Fund)"
WWF UK is a registered charity number 201707;
page 80, The Scouting Association;
page 89, Dundee Tourist Board;
page 100, Dr C Etzlstorfer, University of Linz, and Tanni Grey,
British Wheelchair Racing Association.

Contents

Introduction

The aim of this book is to provide teachers throughout the UK with a set of largely self-supporting and fun activities, which can be 'dipped into' throughout the year. These activities are designed for children with a wide range of abilities and reflect aspects of every subject within the primary curriculum, as well as the cross-curricular themes.

The book is divided into sections according to the months of the year. Each section begins with a diary page where the children can record home or school events (for example, birthdays or homework) or other special or historical dates. It then offers activities based on festivals, the seasons and famous events or people. The final section contains sheets that could be used at various times in the year.

The dates of many festivals are calculated by their religious observers according to non-Gregorian calendars, and so appear to vary within the Western year. In this book, such 'moveable feasts' occur towards the end of the section for the first month in which they may occur. For example, the Chinese New Year may fall in January or February, so its activity is found on page 19 in the 'January' section. The exact date of a festival in any one year can be found in the annual *Shap Calendar of Religious Festivals* (Shap Working Party c/o The National Society's RE Centre, 36 Causton Street, London, SW1P 4AU).
❏ denotes suggestions for extension activities.

About the authors

Phil Newton teaches at Knowsley Northern Primary Support Centre, a school for children with moderate learning difficulties.
Lynda Richardson has responsibility for SEN at Eastcroft Primary School, Kirkby, Merseyside.

January

New Year's resolutions Encourage the children to make resolutions by presenting your own.
❏ Award a certificate, designed by the children, to people who fulfil their resolutions.
The first top hat Record the class's ideas that could contribute to a design on the board. For example, for 'a beach party hat' suggestions might include a sand-castle or a surfboard.
Fairy-tales The children should use minimal text. You could provide key words to be included.
❏ Devise favourite fairy-tale cartoon strips.
Facing symmetry Initially discuss 'symmetrical'. Let the children make a rough draft of the faces first. Other collage materials could be used.
Queen Victoria The NC for history encourages considering Victorian changes to transport.
Answers: TT, 'I'm glad...'; Lady M, 'Wonderful!...'; Mr G, 'Jolly good!...'; SB, 'Oh no!...'.
❏ Discuss the consequences of more modern developments, such as aeroplanes or computer technology. Consider different opinions.
Wolfgang Amadeus Mozart You may need to define the types of musical instruments first.
Answers: strings – double bass, piano, violin; brass – trumpet, tuba; woodwind – clarinet, saxophone; percussion – drums, tambourine, triangle.
Tu b'Shevat
Answers: 1. roots; 2. bark; 3. leaves; 4. trunk; 5. branches.
❏ The children could collect and identify various of leaves, describing their shapes and textures.
Chinese New Year
❏ Can the children find out the significance for the Chinese of the colour red?
Snow people
❏ Discuss winter in the southern hemisphere – beach B-B-Q Christmas dinner, for example!

Teachers' Notes

February

Sir Robert Peel
Answers: 2; 1; 3.
❏ Let the children write to the local police to ask about their uniforms and the technology they use.
Cigarette advertising Leaflets on the effects of smoking, from doctors' surgeries and local health promotion clinics, may be useful.
❏ Some of the speeches could be redrafted as letters to be sent off to cigarette companies.
The senses It may be useful to have a selection of objects available, similar to those listed.
❏ The children could collect other objects to identify by touch, sound or taste only.
Alexander Selkirk The story of *Robinson Crusoe* was inspired by Alexander Selkirk's experiences. The children should use all the items mentioned on the page in their stories and plan an ending.
Newscasting Discuss why women were not considered for such TV posts previously. Do the children think verbal skills are gender-based?
❏ Start a 'job spot'. Make lists of skills needed for particular jobs. Challenge gender stereotypes.
Decimal currency Real coins may be needed.
Answers: 1. 26p, 58p, 32p, 44p; 2. drinks bill; 3. fruit bill; 4. 84p; 5. £1.60; 6. 12p; 7. 40p.
The planet Pluto As a starting point, describe Earth in the same detailed terms.
International Friendship Day Discuss friendship to generate some key words. Hold a ceremony to present the completed certificates, but make sure that every child receives a 'diploma'.
Shrove Tuesday Explain Lent and 'fasting'. It would be advisable for an adult to 'flip' the pancakes over. Remind the class about hygiene – clean hands, work surfaces and equipment.

March

The beginning of spring
Answers: hen – chick; frog – tadpole; cow – calf; duck – duckling; butterfly – caterpillar; cat – kitten; tiger – cub; dog – puppy.

Saint David's Day
Answers: 1. Christian crucifix; 2. telephone; 3. disabled access; 4. Campaign for Nuclear Disarmament (organisation against nuclear arms); 5. wash programme/temperature; 6. Jewish Star of David; 7. wiring diagram for a plug; 8. Roman numeral for 3; 9. male and female access; 10. parking allowed.
❑ Identify any uses of signs around school.

Wind in the Willows
Discuss the characters from some favourite books; what makes them interesting? How does the author describe them?
❑ The children could write a story involving the new characters they have described.

Alexander Graham Bell
Consider the contribution new technology makes to our lives. How do the children think people communicated before the telephone was invented?
❑ Give pairs of children situations around which to build conversations using toy telephones; for example, following a road accident or talking about a new baby or with a long-lost relative.

Harriet Tubman
Discuss what things the children might feel or notice or do that they could not if they were captive slaves.
❑ Discuss why someone would risk his or her life to help others.

Marcel Marceau
This activity would be more successful done in the school hall or outside (weather permitting). Introduce the activity by miming situations for the class to identify.
❑ Mime games, like 'Give us a clue', could be devised using the TV page from a newspaper to provide programme titles as mime subjects.

Stamps
If possible, invite a stamp collector into school. However, the Post Office produces presentation packs and school materials. Their criteria when choosing stamp designs are: the design must work at stamp size, and individually or as a set; the set must be similar in scale and style, but must have an easily-spotted difference between each stamp; the stamps must always include the monarch's head at the top, looking in, and the stamp's value, and cannot feature living people, except the Royal family.
❑ The children could try to extend their designs to full sets of stamps. This is much harder.

The washing machine
The children should focus on the changes in technology and the influence of electricity on domestic appliances.
Answers: 2; 3; 1.
❑ They could devise a questionnaire about the types of cleaning technology used in the home. Do the people answering remember or know of any earlier equipment which did the same jobs?

Vincent Van Gogh
A print of *The Bedroom* (*1888*) would be useful to inspire the children. Alternatively, collect a number of 'restful' objects for discussion and sketching; for example, cushions, books, music or even plants.

Mothering Sunday
When completed, the certificates should be cut out and mounted.

Easter
The children could decide on a theme for their eggs. Hold a competition where they can vote anonymously for the most original design.

Passover
Initially, tell the children the story of Moses. They could go on to include religious, sporting or political leaders in their lists. Encourage them to consider culture and gender.

April

April Fool's Day
Talk about April Fool's tricks which the children have experienced.

Discuss categories of news to stimulate ideas.
❑ The children could 'broadcast' their tricks.

The Boat Race
The children will need to understand the use of scale.
Answers: 9m; 18m; 6m; 6m; 9m; 20 minutes.

The modern Olympic games
Discuss this sheet prior to the PE lesson. If possible, use a circuit system where the children rotate tasks.

World Health Organisation
Cut out, sort and display further pictures of foods from magazines.
❑ The children could compile a data sheet to find out the most popular foods in their class.

The *Titanic*
Introduce this activity to the whole class. Then, in groups, let them make considered judgements. Compare and contrast the outcomes.

Play school
This is a Key Stage 1 activity.
Answers: 7 squares; 7 triangles; 8 circles.
❑ Discuss other children's TV programmes. Which are the children's favourites and why?

The one pound coin
Provide a selection of modern coins and notes, including foreign currency, for the children to look at. Compare and discuss the information found on money.
Answer:

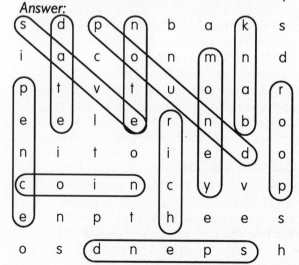

❑ What would the children do with one million pounds? Ask them to write down their ideas.

William Shakespeare This activity explores Shakespeare's diverse mastery of language from a light-hearted starting point. Select some everyday objects to inspire discussion. The children should consider what would make the objects useless, such as a pencil being blunt. Then this becomes the jibe; 'You blunt pencil!'

❑ Discuss, and encourage the children to write about, the causes and results of name-calling.

The water cycle

Answers (in order): Sun; evaporation; water vapour; clouds; snow; hail; rain; pollution; sea.

❑ The children could name and record cloud coverage: cirrus – wispy cloud; stratus – high sheet-like cloud; cumulus – small, fluffy, drifting cloud; nimbostratus – rain and storm cloud.

May

The Channel Tunnel The children could write captions reflecting the points of view of the investors, the British and French governments, the ferry workers and travellers regarding the Channel Tunnel. A free publications catalogue is available from: Eurotunnel Exhibition Centre, St Martin's Plain, Folkestone, Kent CT19 4QD.

❑ Collect brochures to compare travelling by train through the tunnel and travelling by ferry.

The end of World War II The children could research Winston Churchill's actual speech.

❑ Use the speeches as a basis for role-play about receiving the news that the war is over.

The Red Cross The children could prepare questions about the professions in the activity in letters or for a pre-arranged interview, in order to find out more about their community work.

Stevie Wonder Use this sheet to evaluate the children's compositions or pre-recorded music.

❑ Stevie Wonder is blind. Discuss how this might help or hamper his composing.

The Oscars Encourage the children to make their design encompass the theme chosen, or suggest classmates or celebrities for whom to design awards. Then hold an awards ceremony.

Everest expedition Start by talking about Mount Everest's location (Nepal, E. Himalayas), height (29,028 feet) and conditions (often below 0°C).

Helen Sharman The children should consider what evidence the 'alien' would need to prove the existence of life on Earth.

❑ The children could list questions which they might ask about habitation on another planet.

Tomb treasures If the children know about Ancient Egypt they could select historical items, such as statues of the gods, furniture, food or *shabtis* (figures who 'did the work' in the Afterlife).Or they could select modern items.

June

Queen Elizabeth II The children could design traditional crowns or use a theme such as 'Britain'.

World Environment Day The class should consider and emphasise their aims as 'Green Teams' against pollution and for conservation.

❑ By attaching a safety pin to a circular piece of card, and sticking on or copying their designs, the children could make real badges.

D-Day This activity requires an atlas.

Answers: 1. Paris; 2. Mediterranean; 3. Luxembourg; 4. Alps; 5. a. France, b. Germany, c. England; 6. Lisbon; 7. a. Denmark, b. Greece, c. Scotland.

❑ Can the children devise their own Europe quiz?

Charles Dickens Encourage the children to work on rhyming couplets. A list of key food words may be useful for some children.

The twenty pence coin Real coins may help the children to complete these questions.

Answers: 12p; 14p; 12p; 6p; 11p; 20p; 20p; 20p.

Wild things Discuss the importance of safety and conservation when doing a minibeast hunt. Let only one person (probably the teacher) move and replace things, such as leaves and soil, in order to see and collect minibeasts.

Emmeline Pankhurst Women in Britain were not allowed to vote in political elections until 1918, when the suffragettes won the vote for women over 30. In 1928, women over 21 were given the vote.

The first woman in space The children may need additional reference books in order to answer these questions.

Answers: 1. Sun; 2. Mars; 3. Saturn; 4. Mercury; 5. Uranus; 6. Pluto; 7. Jupiter; 8. Venus; 9. Sun; 10. Neptune; 11. nine.

Father's Day If some children do not live with their fathers, offer opportunities to make the card as a thank-you for someone special. White out the logo before photocopying, so that the children can write in the name of the recipient.

Wimbledon The children should plot the rainfall using small crosses. For rain gauges, plastic bottles (with the top third cut off and inverted into the bottle) and millimetre strips would be useful.

Answers: 6; 3 and 7; 3 and 7; 6; 9mm; 3mm.

July

Live Aid Talk about why people organise charity events such as 'Comic Relief Day'. Have some LP or CD covers available to inspire the children.

Disneyland In describing the routes, the children should give the direction, using the compass points, and the location, using the street names.

❑ Try some local route planning using OS maps.

The first man on the Moon Give the children information about Mars and/or encourage them to use reference books. Known as the 'red planet', Mars is only half the size of the Earth.

It has the largest volcano in the Solar System, but its temperature never rises above 0°C.
❏ The children could make models of their spacecrafts.

Saint Christopher St Christopher was a third-century Christian martyr. Legend says that he was once required to carry the child Jesus Christ across a river, and feared they would both drown because the child carried with him such a great weight – all the evil in the world. Hence St Christopher is the patron saint of travellers.

Talk about transport today, and investigate local modes of transport using the survey. The children may find it easier to work in pairs: one recording, by using tallying, and one observing.
❏ Carry out a class survey to find out how everybody travels to school.

Henry Ford Consider the materials chosen for particular functions. For example, rubber is used for wheels because it is hard-wearing but flexible. Go on to consider the car's interior.
❏ Let the children design their own car and label the parts and materials used.

Robert Baden-Powell Explain that 'proficiency' is about 'being good at something' and that to earn a badge, the Scouts have to meet certain criteria and be assessed successfully.
❏ The children could devise proficiency badges to be earned through school work.

Raksha bandhan This activity encourages the children to examine behaviour and co-operation. They may suggest establishing a system of taking turns and not discriminating by gender.
❏ Make *rakhi* using plaited red and yellow wool.

Summer holidays The children will need atlases to locate the countries. Brochures may be useful when identifying the landmarks.
Answers: 1. Egypt, Sphinx and the Pyramids; 2. France, Eiffel Tower; 3. Greece, Parthenon;

4. USA, Statue of Liberty; 5. Australia, Sydney Opera House; 6. India, Taj Mahal; 7. England, Big Ben and Houses of Parliament.

Here comes summer! The children should record the differences by writing, for example 'deck-chair pattern', and by circling the items.
Answers:

Flowers It would be useful if some real flowers could be available for the children to examine.
Answers: 1. anthers; 2. ovaries; 3. petals; 4. ovules.

August

Alexander Fleming
Answers: 1. heart; 2. trachea; 3. liver; 4. gall-bladder; 5. stomach; 6. lungs; 7. kidneys.

John McCarthy Discuss why hostages are taken and consider the appropriateness of this in relation to human rights.

Alfred Hitchcock Talk about a thriller being full of mystery, suspense and excitement until the last minute, when a startling revelation 'ties up all the loose ends' and fits all the clues.

The Tay Bridge This activity encourages awareness of differing viewpoints. The factors in developing a new road include: convenience, pollution, conservation and employment.
❏ Role-play a public meeting to discuss the proposal, with the children taking on the roles of characters from the activity page.

Martin Luther King, jun. Martin Luther King, jun. was a Baptist minister and civil rights activist. His vision for America was of a place of equality, without discrimination because of skin colour.
❏ Discuss cultural differences, and how these are distorted by prejudice.

Vacuum cleaner Encourage imaginative designs, for example robots or machines.
❏ Suggest the children investigate the technology available to do domestic work in the home and identify 'gaps in the market'.

September

The Great Fire of London The children should mention the changes in pumps (hand to electrically powered), protective clothing and engines (horse to mechanically powered).
❏ Examine the fire precautions taken in school.

The first library Discuss why we have public libraries and the types of books and reference materials available to borrowers, including CDs, details of local events and maps.
❏ The children could devise a readers' guide on how to use non-fiction materials, including using the contents and index and scanning the text.

The first SOS broadcast The children could tap out their messages on the tabletop rather than using an electric circuit with a bulb.
❏ Can the children describe situations where the Morse code would be useful?

Jesse Owens The questions could explore: training and diet; Jesse's feelings when he received the gold medals; and how he relaxed.
❏ Help the children to consider Hitler's anger at Jesse Owens' success in the 1936 Olympics, when his white 'master race' were beaten by a talented black athlete.

Book review You will need to offer a selection of stories appropriate for the children in the class.

Include some by Roald Dahl, if possible. Store the reviews beside the books to which they refer.

Agatha Christie With the class, brainstorm skills which are important for a good investigator. Make a list of key words; for example, 'nosy' or 'resourceful'. A thesaurus would be useful here.

Autumn leaves This could be a relatively self-supporting counting activity for R/Y1 children.

The marathon The current world record running marathon times are: men 02:06:50 and women 02:21:06. Point out to the children that world record wheelchair marathon times are much quicker: men 01:22:12 and women 01:42:00. These times may be reduced further – can the children check/find out the latest records? They will need to understand the 24 hour clock for this activity. They may find clock-faces useful.
Answers: 17:36 (2nd); 18:41 (8th); 17:28 (1st); 19:00 (9th); 18:15 (7th); 20:02 (10th); 17:37 (3rd); 18:03 (5th); 17:46 (4th).

Back to school The children could create a number of designs and make a final selection to draw on to the models. When designing their badges, the children should consider what is significant about their school and its principles.

October

The first postcard Provide real holiday post-cards and brochures as inspiration. Alternatively, the children could create an imaginary location, offering facilities such as a theme park, free ice-cream and swimming pools with fun slides.
❏ The children could draw pictures of their destinations for the fronts of their postcards.

Fast food
❏ The children could use telephone directories to compile a list of the different types of fast food restaurants in their area, and conduct a survey to find out which are the most popular.

Hairstyles Provide magazines and catalogues showing examples of different hairstyles. Encourage the children to design 'alternative' hairstyles; not necessarily ones they have seen.

The first motor omnibus Look at a selection of magazine advertisements. Discuss why a bus is a good place to advertise, and how and why advertisers make their products more appealing.

Potato crisps Have a selection of crisps for the children to taste. Can they identify the flavours of the crisps by taste alone? *Always be aware of possible food allergies among the children before trying any tasting activity.*

Electricity Remind the children of the dangers of thunderstorms and the correct safety precautions should they be caught out in one.
Answer: there are 13 uses of electricity shown.
❏ Can the children think of any more uses of electricity which could have been included on a whole-household picture?

United Nations Day The children could consider images associated with peace, harmony, co-operation, world unity and so on.

Hallowe'en The children could produce their writing as a story about being lost in a grave-yard at night. Encourage them to use the picture to enhance their use of descriptive language.

Harvest festival
Answers (in order): sowing; wheat growing; harvesting; flour mill; baking bread; delivering bread; child buying bread; child eating bread.

Autumn apple appetisers Carefully supervise the apple coring and cooking. Tell Hallowe'en stories while the apples are being eaten.

November

All Saints' Day
Answer (in order): Jesus was carrying the cross...; Then Veronica came...; Veronica took off her veil...; Jesus thanked Veronica with a smile; Veronica left and went home; At home, Veronica looked at her veil ... .

Bonfire Night Brainstorm about the things that the children will see, hear, taste, smell and touch on Bonfire Night. Encourage them to complete the poem in rhyming (or not) couplets.

Basketball
Answers – skills suggested might be: accuracy, communication, sportsmanship, co-ordination, agility and co-operation. A team captain should be: supportive, committed, fair-minded, a good listener, encouraging and positive.

Buried treasure
Answers: treasure D5; ship C2; quicksand C3; shark D5; palm trees D4; skull and crossbones D2.
❏ The children could use squared paper to create their own treasure maps.

Family trees The pictures should be organised so that Queen Elizabeth, The Queen Mother, is at the top, then HM The Queen and Prince Philip, then Charles with Diana, Anne, Andrew and Edward, then Prince William and Prince Henry.
❏ Can the children identify The Queen Mother's husband (George V) and add him to the tree? The children could bring in photographs to make their own family trees. Handle this sensitively, considering the issues of separated parents.

The first hot-air balloon
❏ The children could also consider where they would like to travel to and write an itinerary.

Diwali Light candles to inspire the children. For safety, use night-lights in a sand tray and keep matches out of the children's reach.
❏ This festival also commemorates the return of Rama and Sita to their kingdom after 14 years in exile. Make shadow puppets to retell this story.

Feed the birds The children will need to be supervised when melting the lard.

❏ Encourage them to design other ways of feeding the birds, such as a bird table.

Bird-watcher's diary To make identification easier, let the children use reference materials and colour in the bird pictures on the chart prior to making the observations.

December

Walt Disney First talk about cartoon characters the children know and answer the questions on the page for each of these.
❏ The children could use their new cartoon characters in a cartoon strip.

The first heart transplant Initially, the children will need to practise measuring their pulses. They should exercise under close adult supervision. Add the duration of the exercise to the sheet before photocopying it; the activity must only continue long enough to raise the children's pulse rate significantly. Talk about how we use more energy when we are exercising , so the heart pumps faster to distribute extra oxygen around the body in the blood.
❏ What is the average resting pulse rate in the class? Why do the children think that some people's pulses are much slower (or faster)?

The first motorway
❏ Survey other children or adults for their views on the advantages and disadvantages of motorways.

Saint Nicholas St Nicholas, the patron saint of children, was the fourth-century bishop of Myra (in modern Turkey). He was made a saint for his miracles and good deeds; traditionally he is said to have dropped gold for the dowries of three poor sisters down their chimney. Dutch settlers took the tradition of *Sinter Klass* to America, where he came to be called Santa Claus and his visits became a Christmas Eve tradition.

In their letters the children could say why they think they deserve some presents and what they would like. Also, they could request gifts for their families. Encourage them to list their choices and then prioritise them for the letter.

Big Ben First revise how to write digital time.
❏ The children could write a report on 'The day time stood still', perhaps including the consequences that they have identified.

Beethoven Discuss the types of percussion instruments (such as shakers or scrapers).
❏ The children could explore different themes when devising their own music; for example, sun, rain, storm, snow or the wind.

The Christmas story If the children are familiar with the Christmas story, remove the list of keywords before photocopying the sheets. *Answers* (in order): Gabriel; Jesus; Joseph; Bethlehem; inn; stable; Mary; manger; angel; shepherds; three kings; star; gold; frankincense; myrrh.

Hanukkah This eight-day Jewish festival of light is held to commemorate the Jewish victory over the Emperor of Syria in 175 BCE. After ten years, the Jews reclaimed their temple in Jerusalem and lit the temple lamp to show God's presence. There was only enough oil for one day, but the lamp stayed alight for eight days! Today the festival is celebrated with *menorah* candles, with parties with special food, especially *latkes* (fried potato pancakes), and by playing the 'Dreidel game'.

All year round

Hijra Muslim festivals are fixed in the Muslim calendar, but the Muslim lunar year is 11 days shorter than the Gregorian solar year. Thus, Muslim festivals *appear* to move 'backwards' 11 days in each Western year. Check the exact date annually in the *Shap Calendar of Religious Festivals*.

For their new town, the children should consider facilities for leisure, work, shopping, transport and housing. Encourage them to consider different age groups and religions.
❏ The children could draw plans of their towns.

All about me Stimulate ideas by sharing some of your personal characteristics.

All about my work Use this sheet on Open Evenings to show the topics covered in the year.

All about my holiday To promote discussion, first discuss what you did during the holidays.
❏ The children could add a section on what they would have liked to have done.

Year round quiz This activity will help you to assess the children's knowledge of the order of the months and of seasonal weather patterns.

Weather headlines Discuss the types and effects of adverse weather. Let the children jot down their ideas on the back of the sheet before drafting their reports. If possible, let them use the computer to give their final reports the feel of a 'proper' newspaper.

Weather watch This activity encourages the children to describe the differences between summer and winter weather conditions.

Weather symbols 1 and 2 Cut out and mount the symbols for the children to use in weather reports, or display them next to a calendar or date sign or on a map of the UK.

The temperature and sun symbols should have red figures on a yellow background. The raindrop shapes should be dark blue. The thunderstorm symbol should have a black cloud and a yellow flash, and the windspeed symbol should be black with the speed written in white.

Spring, Summer, Autumn, Winter These sheets provide opportunities to present writing on seasonal or 'all year round' subjects, such as poetry, diaries or nature notes, in an attractive way.

January

1	18
2	19
3	20
4	21
5	22
6	23
7	24
8	25
9	26
10	27
11	28
12	29
13	30
14	31
15	**Notes**
16	
17	**Birthdays**

Name _____

New Year's resolutions

At the beginning of the new year, people sometimes take a fresh look at themselves. They look forward and set themselves goals, called resolutions, for the year ahead.

✤ Think about the things that you would like to achieve this year at home and at school and make some of your own New Year's resolutions.

✤ Write your ideas in the football shapes below.

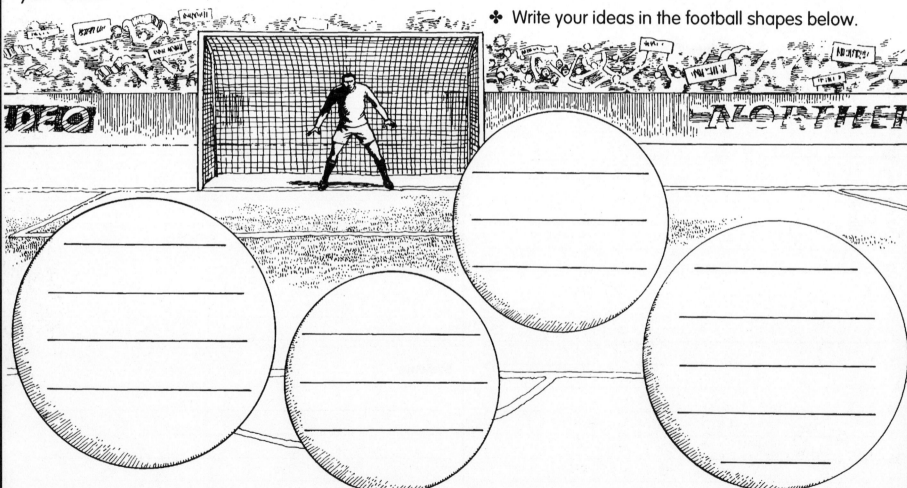

The first top hat

On 5 January 1797, in London, a man called John Hetherington wore the first top hat and was arrested by the police who thought that the hat might frighten people.

♣ Design a hat to wear for a special occasion. Here are some ideas:
- a beach party;
- the opening of a zoo;
- a wedding ceremony;
- the opening of a sweet factory.

♣ Maybe you could make up your own special occasion.

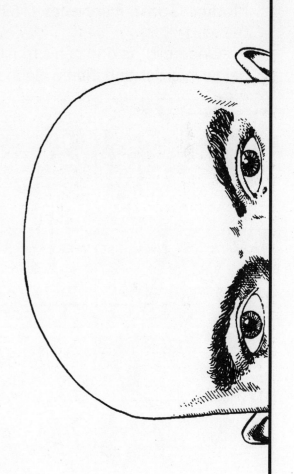

Name _____

Fairy-tales

Charles Perrault was born on 12 January 1628. He was the author of the Mother Goose Fairy-tales (1697).

♣ 'Cinderella', is one of his most famous fairy-tales. Put the pictures below in order and then write the story.

Facing symmetry

Paul Cézanne, a famous French artist, was born on 19 January 1839. He was famous for his 'geometric' paintings. Geometry involves the use of shape.

You will need: two pieces of card in contrasting colours, paper, pencil, scissors and adhesive.

✤ Follow these instructions to construct a symmetrical face picture.

• Take one piece of card and draw on half a face shape.

• Put the piece of contrasting coloured card underneath and cut through both, so that you can make a full face shape.

• Stick the two half face shapes down on the paper.

• Use the rest of the card to make features. For example, if you were using blue and yellow card, a blue eye would go on the yellow half of the face and a yellow eye would go on the blue half and so on.

• The card for the hair can be curled to create a three-dimensional effect.

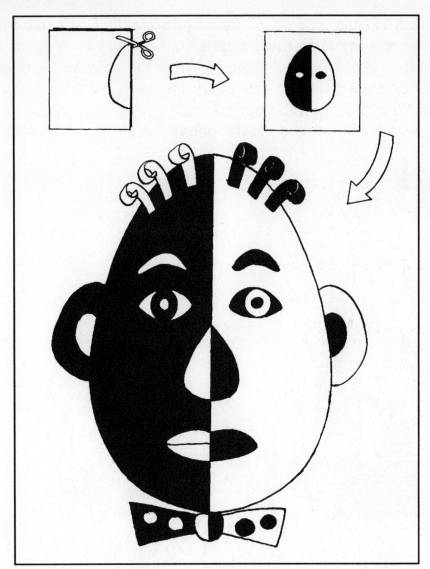

Name _____

Queen Victoria

Queen Victoria died on 22 January 1901; she had ruled Britain for 63 years.
During her reign there were lots of changes in everyday life. One of the areas of change was transport. When the railways were introduced people had different points of view about them.

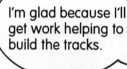

♣ Match each caption to the person whom you think might have said it.

Jolly good! I can make more money by sending the clothes we make to be sold all over the country.

Oh no! All of us workers will be out of a job because the trains can travel faster than we can.

I'm glad because I'll get work helping to build the tracks.

Wonderful! Now I can get to London so much faster to visit the theatre and do lots more shopping.

**Tommy Tippins
(Labourer)**

**Lady Muck of
Muck Hall**

**Mr Grabbit
(Factory owner)**

**Sally Butler
(Canal barge worker)**

Name _____

Wolfgang Amadeus Mozart

On 27 January 1756 the great composer Mozart was born. He could play the piano when he was four years old and was composing his own music by the time he was five. During his lifetime, Mozart composed over 600 pieces of music for orchestras.

♣ Opposite are pictures of some of the different instruments. Sort them into the correct section of either woodwind, brass, strings or percussion.

Section	Instruments
brass	
percussion	
woodwind	
strings	

violin

tuba

drums

trumpet

saxophone

triangle

clarinet

piano

tambourine

double bass

Tu b'Shevat

Tu b'Shevat

The Jewish feast day of Tu b'Shevat, which marks the end of the heavy rain period in Israel, is held in January or February, on the fifteenth day of the Jewish month of Shevat. During this festival, children plant trees to celebrate the beginning of the time of new growth.

♣ Label the parts of this tree.

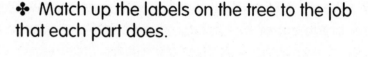

♣ Match up the labels on the tree to the job that each part does.

1. [   ] Take in water from the ground to support the tree.

2. [   ] Protects the tree from damage by the weather and animals.

3. [   ] Grow during spring and summer, but sometimes fall off in winter. Use sunlight to make food.

4. [   ] Supports the tree and transports water and food throughout it.

5. [   ] Take water from the trunk to the leaves and food from the leaves to the trunk.

Name _____

Chinese New Year

Chinese New Year is celebrated in late January or early February, depending on the date of the first full moon. The celebrations last for two weeks. During the festival, lanterns are hung along the streets and there is a parade with dancing and music. A huge dragon, with people inside, collects presents of money, which are hung outside shops in red envelopes.

♣ Follow these instructions to make a Chinese lantern.

You will need: a piece of decorated paper, a piece of double-sided red paper, scissors and adhesive.

2cm gap

2cm gap

• Stick a piece of paper decorated with your own design on to a larger piece of double-sided red paper.

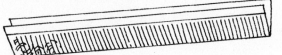

fold

• Fold the paper in half and draw lines, about 1cm apart, from the fold up to the edge of the decorated paper.

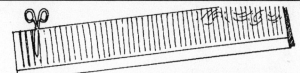

• Cut along the lines.
Do NOT cut past the decorated paper.

• Open out the paper and fold it round so that the shorter edges overlap and then stick them together.

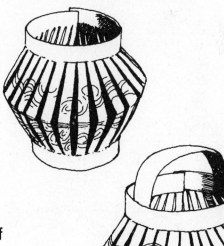

• For a handle, cut a strip of red paper about 2cm wide. Stick the handle on to the top of the lantern.

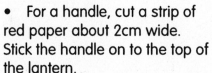

Snow people

Name _____

Snow people

January is the first month of the year and is one of the coldest.

❖ Put these things on this snow person:
- 3 red buttons;
- 2 blue eyes;
- 1 pink nose;
- 1 brown mouth;

❖ Colour the scarf blue.

❖ Colour the hat green.

❖ Put these things on this snow person:
- 4 green buttons;
- 2 brown eyes;
- 1 red nose;
- 1 pink mouth;

❖ Colour the scarf orange.

❖ Colour the hat yellow.

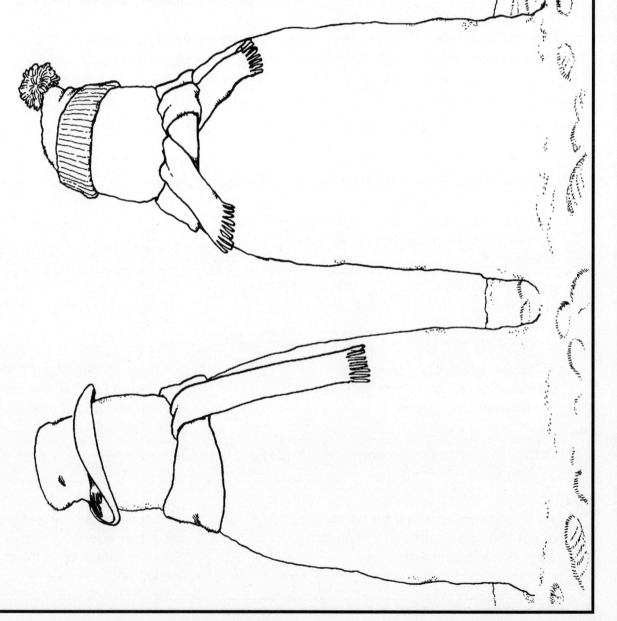

February

1	18
2	19
3	20
4	21
5	22
6	23
7	24
8	25
9	26
10	27
11	28
12	29
13	
14	**Notes**
15	
16	**Birthdays**
17	

Name _____

Sir Robert Peel

Robert Peel was born on 5 February 1788. He founded the police force in Britain in 1829. Early police officers were called 'peelers' or 'bobbies'.

♣ Look at the pictures below. They show police officers in their uniforms.

♣ Put the pictures in chronological order.

♣ Opposite, describe how the uniform has changed or stayed the same.

Cigarette advertising

On 8 February 1965 cigarette advertising was banned from British television.

♣ Write a speech saying why you think cigarette advertising should be banned completely.

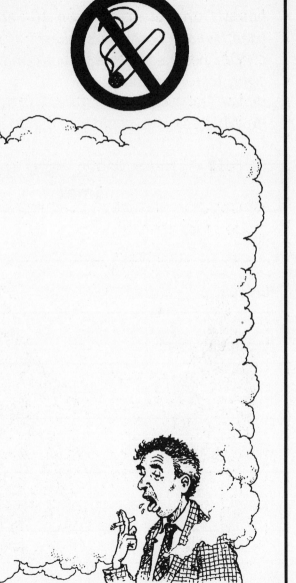

The senses

Name _____

The senses

Jimmy Durante was born on 10 February 1893. He became a famous comedian who used his long nose in his jokes!

Our nose, ears, eyes, mouth and hands allow us to use our senses of smell, hearing, sight, taste and touch.

♣ Which senses could you use to identify each of these things? Tick the correct box.

	Smell	Hearing	Sight	Taste	Touch
music					
fresh air					
hamburger					
flower					
wind					
bread					
rain					

Alexander Selkirk

On 12 February 1709 Alexander Selkirk was rescued from a desert island where he had been stranded for five years.

♣ Imagine that you are the captain of the good ship *Lollipop*, and that you have been left stranded on 'Dinosaur Island'. All you have with you is your knife, a telescope, some rope, a pen and paper and a lollipop! What happens next?

Newscasting

Newscasting

On 13 February 1978 Anna Ford became ITN's first female newscaster.

✤ Imagine that there has been a fire in your school. Pretend that you are reporting the events on the television news and write your script below. You might include interviews, what people said, details of how the fire started, who raised the alarm and information about any damage or injuries. Turn the page over if you need more room.

✤ Share your report with the class.

Script

Hello, this is _____ with the news.

Today, the staff and children of _____ School had a lucky escape.

_____

_____

_____

_____

_____

_____

_____

_____

Decimal currency

On 15 February 1971 decimal currency was introduced. This meant that there were 100 pence in one pound. New coins had to be minted. Before this, there were 240d, or 240 old pennies, in one pound.

✤ Here are some money problems. Look at the shopping bills below.

✤ Now answer these questions.
- What is the total cost of the items on each bill?
- Which bill was the most expensive?
- Which bill was the cheapest?
- How much were the fruit bill and drink bill together?
- How much did all the bills cost together?
- How much more was the bill for the comics than the bill for the sweets?
- After the shopping trip, how much change was left if you started with £2.00?

✤ Make up some questions of your own using these bills and test a friend.

Comics
Deano 22p
Whizzer 22p

total _____

Fruit
apple 7p
banana 6p
grapes 5p
pear 8p

total _____

Drinks
coffee 20p
milk 14p
coke 14p
lemonade 10p

total _____

Sweets
crisps 12p
nuts 10p
chews 5p
gum 5p

total _____

Name _____

The planet Pluto

On 18 February 1930 Clyde W. Tombaugh, an astronomer from Arizona, discovered the planet Pluto. Pluto is the smallest of the planets in our Solar System and is 5,970 million kilometres from the Sun. (Wow!)

♣ Imagine you have landed on a newly discovered planet.

♣ Describe the planet. Think about the vegetation, the landscape and any life-forms.

Captain's log...

International Friendship Day

International Friendship Day is celebrated on 19 February. It is a day when we can acknowledge and show how much we appreciate our friends.

✤ Present your special friend with a 'Friendship diploma' listing all their good qualities.

Friendship diploma

Awarded to _____ *by* _____

The following qualities make you a special friend:

_____

_____

_____

_____

Date _____ *Signed* _____

Shrove Tuesday

Name _____

Shrove Tuesday

The 40 days before Easter, when some Christians fast (go without food) and pray, is called 'Lent'. Shrove Tuesday is the day before Lent starts, and can fall in February or March. Traditionally, people eat pancakes on Shrove Tuesday to use up food before they start to fast in Lent.

✤ Follow these instructions to make your own pancakes.
You will need an adult to help you!

You will need:
100g flour
1 beaten egg
250ml milk
salt
sugar
lemon juice
cooking oil
sieve
mixing bowl
frying pan
wooden spoon
plate
knife and fork

1 Sieve the flour into a mixing bowl with a pinch of salt.
2 Add the beaten egg.
3 Add the milk a little at a time and stir it into the flour.
4 Beat the batter well for about five minutes.
5 Leave the batter to stand for an hour or more.
6 Heat one tablespoonful of oil in the frying pan.
Be careful!
7 Pour in enough batter to cover the base of the pan.
8 Cook the pancake until it is set, then flip it over.
9 When it is brown on both sides, gently slip the pancake on to a plate and sprinkle it with sugar and lemon juice.
10 Enjoy your pancake!

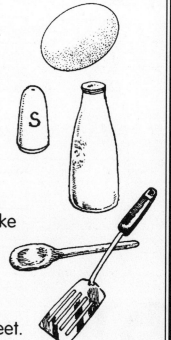

✤ Can you think of other toppings to serve with your pancakes? Plan your new recipes on the back of this sheet.

30

March

1 _____	18 _____
2 _____	19 _____
3 _____	20 _____
4 _____	21 _____
5 _____	22 _____
6 _____	23 _____
7 _____	24 _____
8 _____	25 _____
9 _____	26 _____
10 _____	27 _____
11 _____	28 _____
12 _____	29 _____
13 _____	30 _____
14 _____	31 _____
15 _____	**Notes** _____
16 _____	
17 _____	**Birthdays** _____

The beginning of spring

The beginning of spring

March is the beginning of spring. Hedgehogs wake up from their winter sleep and ewes give birth to their lambs.

♣ Match these adult animals to their young by following the maze.

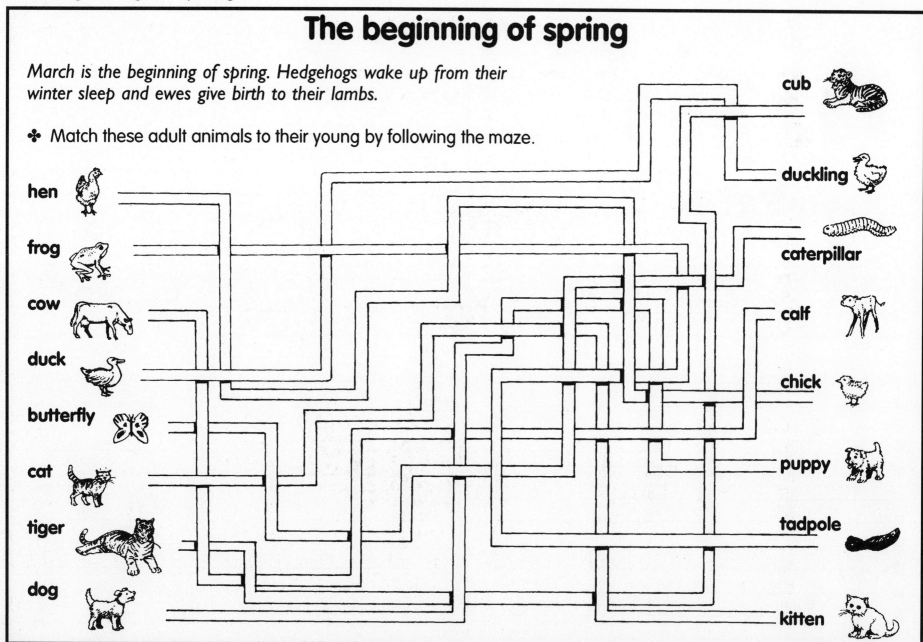

hen

frog

cow

duck

butterfly

cat

tiger

dog

cub

duckling

caterpillar

calf

chick

puppy

tadpole

kitten

Saint David's Day

Saint David's Day is celebrated on 1 March. Saint David is the patron saint of Wales. One symbol for Wales, often worn on Saint David's Day, is the daffodil.

✤ Here are some more symbols which we use in everyday life. What do they mean?

1
2
3
4
5

6
7
8
9
10

✤ Design a symbol for your school. Think about the qualities that are important for your school.

Wind in the Willows

Wind in the Willows

Kenneth Grahame was born on 8 March 1859. He was the author of Wind in the Willows *(1908), a book about the lives of animals on and around a river.*

Before starting to write a story, an author will often plan the personalities of the characters — whether they will be 'goodies' or 'baddies', hardworking or lazy.

♣ Below are some new characters. Can you make up a personality for each of them? Describe what they look like. Where will they live and how will they behave?

Freddy, the frog

_____
_____
_____
_____
_____

Drisella, the duck

_____
_____
_____
_____
_____

Reginald Rat

_____
_____
_____
_____
_____

_____
_____
_____
_____

Alexander Graham Bell

On 10 March 1876 Alexander Graham Bell discovered that the human voice could be transmitted by means of electricity through wires. This was the first step towards the invention of the telephone.

♣ Imagine that you can phone up the inventor of the telephone to tell him why you think it is a good invention. Complete the conversation opposite.

♣ Use your conversation as the basis for a role-play about meeting Alexander Graham Bell.

Mr Bell: Hello.

Me: Oh...hello, this is _____.

Mr Bell: How can I help you?

Me: Well, I was just calling to say...

Harriet Tubman

Harriet Tubman

Harriet Tubman was born as a slave in Maryland, North America, in 1820. She worked on a cotton plantation until 1849 when finally she escaped. Harriet went on to help more than 300 people escape from slavery between 1851 and 1860. She died, aged 93, on 10 March 1913.

♣ This is how Harriet began her description of the sensation of being free. Can you complete her speech?

'The sun came up like gold through the

trees and I felt I was in heaven.....'

Marcel Marceau

22 March is the birthday of Marcel Marceau, a famous French mime artist who was born in 1923. Mime is acting without speech.

♣ Cut out the cards below. Pick a card and mime the actions to your group until they have guessed what you are doing. Then let someone else in your group do the miming.

♣ Make up some cards of your own. Add them to the pack and carry on miming.

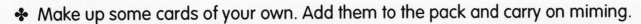

Perform as a clown.	Make a cake.	Conduct an orchestra.	Take photographs at a wedding.

Be a ringmaster at a circus.	Referee a football match.	Plant seeds.	Make a cup of tea.

Name _____

Stamps

On 25 March 1981 the Post Office issued four new stamps for the International Year of the Disabled.

♣ Imagine you have been asked to design some stamps as a celebration for these special occasions: The Olympics; International Book Week, The Year of the Family.

♣ Draw your ideas on the stamp outlines below. Don't forget to include the price of the stamp on your design.

The Olympics

International Book Week

The Year of the Family

The washing machine

The invention of the washing machine, by an American named Nathaniel Briggs, was completed on 28 March 1797.

♣ The pictures below show three methods of washing clothes. Put the methods in chronological order and describe how doing the washing has changed.

_____

_____

_____

_____

_____

_____

_____

_____

_____

_____

_____

_____

Vincent Van Gogh

Vincent Van Gogh

Vincent Van Gogh was a famous painter who was born in the Netherlands on 30 March 1853. The sketch below is in the style of Van Gogh and shows Van Gogh's bedroom in his home at Arles in France (1888–9). He wanted to show 'a feeling of perfect rest'.

♣ Sketch and colour a modern bedroom which you think looks restful and comfortable. Think about: shades of colour, the furniture and the decoration.

Mothering Sunday

The fourth Sunday in Lent, which usually falls in March, is traditionally called 'Mothering Sunday'. It is the day when we all say a special thank you to our mothers for all they do for us.

♣ Fill in the Mothering Sunday certificate below and present it to your mum.

BEST MUM IN THE WORLD CERTIFICATE

Name: _____

For outstanding achievements in: _____

For putting up with: _____

For listening to: _____

My mum is the best mum in the world because: _____

_____

Signed _____

Easter

Easter

Christians believe that Jesus Christ rose from the dead after being crucified. They remember this event on Easter Sunday. Easter Sunday can occur in March or April. Easter eggs are given at this time as a sign of new life.

♣ Create a design for this Easter egg. Give it some 'eggs-traordinary' features! Feet! Ears! Or hair, perhaps!

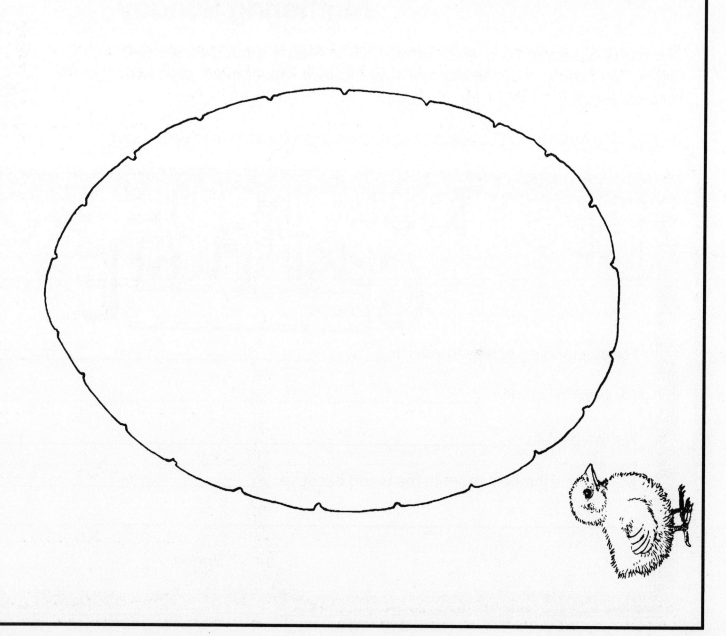

Passover

Passover is a Jewish festival celebrated in late March or early April; the date depends on the new moon. At Passover, Jewish people remember the story of Moses, who led the Israelites out of slavery in Egypt to the 'promised land' of Israel.

♣ Moses was a great leader. What qualities do you think are important for great leaders?

♣ Can you name any other great leaders? Who did they lead? Use the history section of the library to help you.

For example:
Joan of Arc **led** the French army (1429–1431)

_____ **led** _____

_____ **led** _____

_____ **led** _____

_____ **led** _____

Diary page: April

Name _____

April

18	_____
19	_____
20	_____
21	_____
22	_____
23	_____
24	_____
25	_____
26	_____
27	_____
28	_____
29	_____
30	_____

1 _____
2 _____
3 _____
4 _____
5 _____
6 _____
7 _____
8 _____
9 _____
10 _____
11 _____
12 _____
13 _____
14 _____
15 _____
16 _____
17 _____

Notes

_____

_____

Birthdays

_____

_____

_____

April Fool's Day

1 April is April Fool's Day, when people like to play tricks on each other.
    In 1957, as an April Fool's trick, the BBC showed a film on British television where Swiss people were seen to be harvesting spaghetti from trees. People actually rang up wanting to know where they could buy spaghetti plants!

♣ Can you think of an April Fool's trick which could be presented on the television news? Make it as silly as you can.

- Draw it here.

- Explain it here.

Hello, this is the news.

Name _____

The Boat Race

On 4 April 1981 Susan Brown became the first woman to cox the Oxford team in the Boat Race. Oxford won!

♣ Use a ruler to measure the distances on this sketch of our boat race.
It is drawn on a scale of 1cm : 1m.

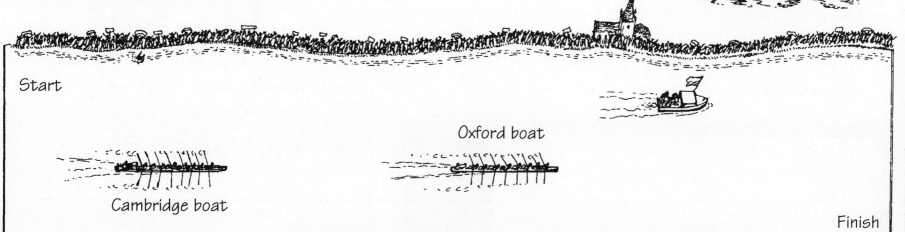

Start

Oxford boat

Cambridge boat

Finish

♣ Now answer these questions.
• How far is the Oxford boat from the finishing line?
• How far is the Cambridge boat from the finishing line?
• What is the distance between the front of the Cambridge boat and the back of the Oxford boat?

• If Oxford won the race by 3m, how much distance did the Cambridge crew make up before the finish?
• The cox sits in the back of the boat. How far is the Cambridge cox from the Oxford cox?
• If it took Oxford five minutes to row a quarter of this race, how long would the race take altogether?

The modern Olympic games

On 6 April 1896 the first modern Olympic games were held in Athens in Greece. To be an Olympic athlete you need to be extremely fit.

♣ Plan a training programme and see whether you can improve your fitness. You may need an adult to help you. Record how many of each of these activities you can complete in 1 minute. Do you get quicker over the weeks?

	Sit-ups	Shuttle runs	Press-ups	Skips	Long jump	Sprint
Week 1						
Week 2						
Week 3						
Week 4						

World Health Organisation

The World Health Organisation was founded on 7 April 1948. Its purpose is to help people all over the world to be healthier.

♣ Use an arrow to match the healthy foods to the smiley face and the unhealthy foods to the sad face.

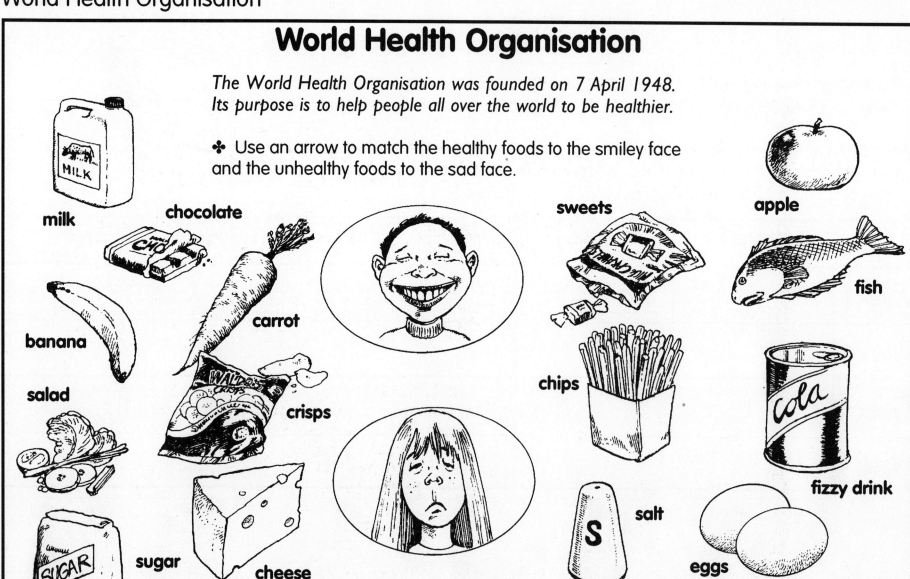

milk

chocolate

carrot

banana

salad

crisps

sugar

cheese

sweets

apple

fish

chips

cola

fizzy drink

salt

eggs

Remember: even healthy foods can be unhealthy if you eat too much of them!

Name _____

The *Titanic*

Disaster struck on 14 April 1912 when the so-called 'unsinkable' ship, the Titanic, hit an iceberg and sank to the bottom of the Atlantic ocean.

♣ Imagine you are on the *Titanic* and are in charge of choosing who will get a place in the last lifeboat. There are only four places left, but there are six people. Who would you choose and why?

Sam Sprinter
A 100 yards runner who holds a world record.

Arthur Sixpence
A pensioner who is a millionaire.

Freda Vote
An enthusiastic campaigner for the suffragettes.

Penny Cillin
A doctor who specialises in cancer research.

Wally Jumper
A 16 year old whose hobby is the new game of basketball.

Paul Forte
A brilliant musician who plays piano all over the world.

I would choose:

1 _____ because _____
_____

2 _____ because _____
_____

3 _____ because _____
_____

4 _____ because _____
_____

Name _____

Play school

On 21 April 1964 BBC2 showed the first ever programme of Play school, an educational series for young children. The presenters used different-shaped windows to introduce parts of the programme. For example, 'How do you think that sweets are made? Let's find out through...the square window.'

♣ Can you sort these shapes into sets?

Colour ☐ in red, △ in green, and ◯ in blue.

♣ How many ☐ are there?

♣ How many △ are there?

♣ How many ◯ are there?

Name _____

The one pound coin

The one pound coin was introduced on 22 April 1983.

♣ Find the following 'money' words in the puzzle below:
pence, coin, date, pound, money, poor, rich, note, save,
bank, spend.

s	d	p	n	b	a	k	s
i	a	c	o	n	m	n	d
p	t	v	t	u	o	a	r
e	e	l	e	r	n	b	o
n	i	t	o	i	e	d	o
c	o	i	n	c	y	v	p
e	n	p	t	h	e	e	s
o	s	d	n	e	p	s	h

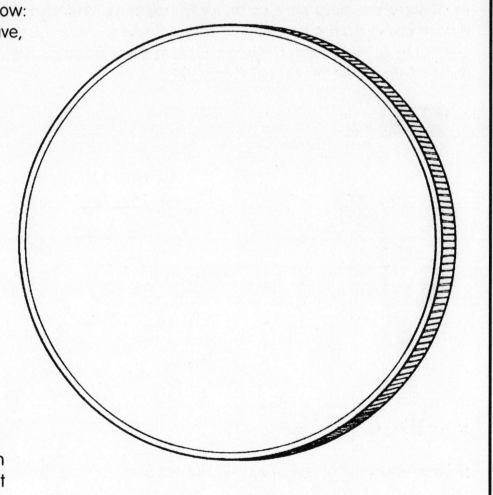

♣ Use the outline opposite to design a new coin with
you as queen or king. Look at any real coin to find out
what else you should put on your coin.

William Shakespeare

Name _____

William Shakespeare

William Shakespeare was a writer. He was born on 23 April 1564, and died on the same day in 1616! He was 52 when he died.

Some of his plays were comedies (funny plays) and some were tragedies (ended sadly). Shakespeare often used unusual words in his plays to poke fun at people. In A Midsummer Night's Dream two characters are arguing, here are some of the things they say to each other:

You painted Maypole!

You bead!

You juggler!

You acorn!

♣ Can you think of any other silly names Shakespeare could have used, such as 'You fluffy pillow!' or 'You overripe tomato!'?
List your ideas on the back of this page.

The water cycle

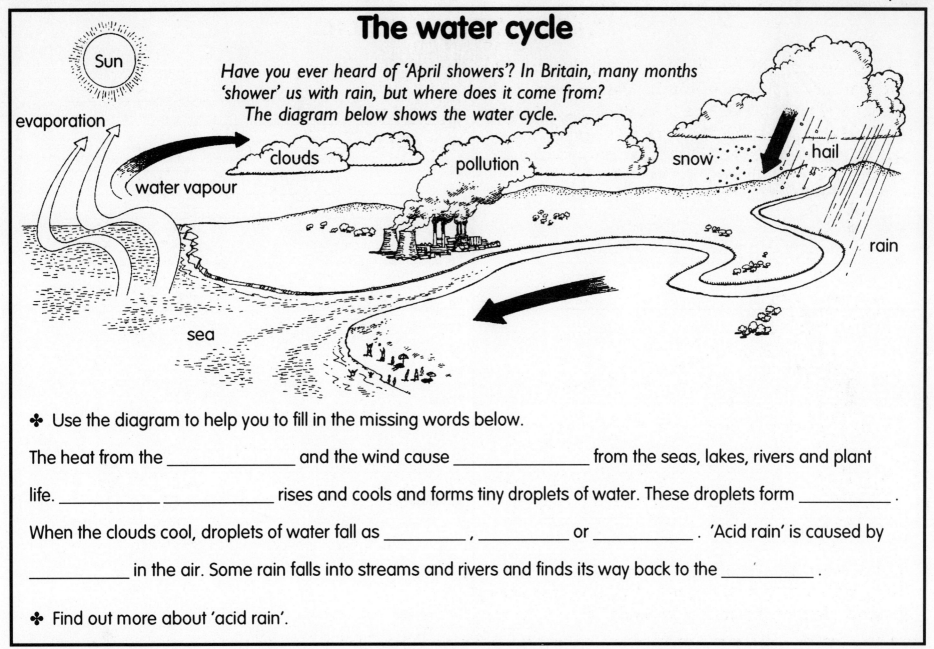

Have you ever heard of 'April showers'? In Britain, many months 'shower' us with rain, but where does it come from? The diagram below shows the water cycle.

Sun

evaporation

water vapour

clouds

pollution

snow

hail

rain

sea

❧ Use the diagram to help you to fill in the missing words below.

The heat from the _____ and the wind cause _____ from the seas, lakes, rivers and plant

life. _____ _____ rises and cools and forms tiny droplets of water. These droplets form _____ .

When the clouds cool, droplets of water fall as _____ , _____ or _____ . 'Acid rain' is caused by

_____ in the air. Some rain falls into streams and rivers and finds its way back to the _____ .

❧ Find out more about 'acid rain'.

Diary page: May

Name _____

May

1 _____	18 _____
2 _____	19 _____
3 _____	20 _____
4 _____	21 _____
5 _____	22 _____
6 _____	23 _____
7 _____	24 _____
8 _____	25 _____
9 _____	26 _____
10 _____	27 _____
11 _____	28 _____
12 _____	29 _____
13 _____	30 _____
14 _____	31 _____
15 _____	**Notes**
16 _____	
17 _____	**Birthdays**

Name _____

The Channel Tunnel

The Channel Tunnel was opened officially on 6 May 1994. It links Britain to France and the rest of Europe by railway.

♣ Read the statements below and say whether they are **fact** or **point of view**.

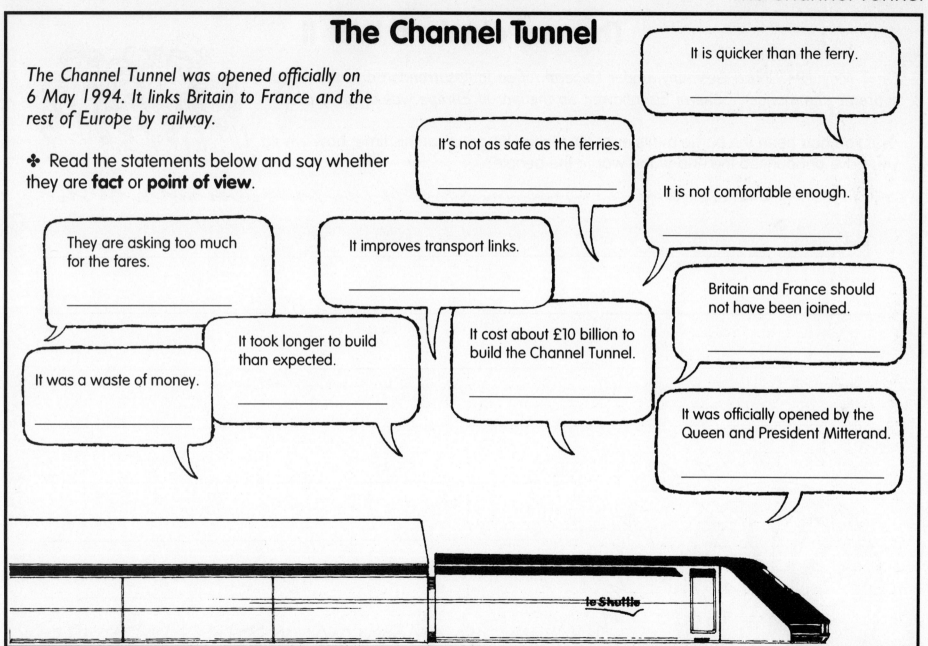

It is quicker than the ferry.

_____

It's not as safe as the ferries.

_____

It is not comfortable enough.

_____

They are asking too much for the fares.

_____

It improves transport links.

_____

Britain and France should not have been joined.

_____

It was a waste of money.

_____

It took longer to build than expected.

_____

It cost about £10 billion to build the Channel Tunnel.

_____

It was officially opened by the Queen and President Mitterand.

_____

Name _____

The end of World War II

On 7 May 1945 Nazi Germany, under General Alfred Jodl, surrendered to the Allied supreme commander, General Eisenhower. So the war in Europe was officially over.

♣ If you had been the prime minister of the United Kingdom at this time, how would you have announced the end of the war to the people?

The Red Cross

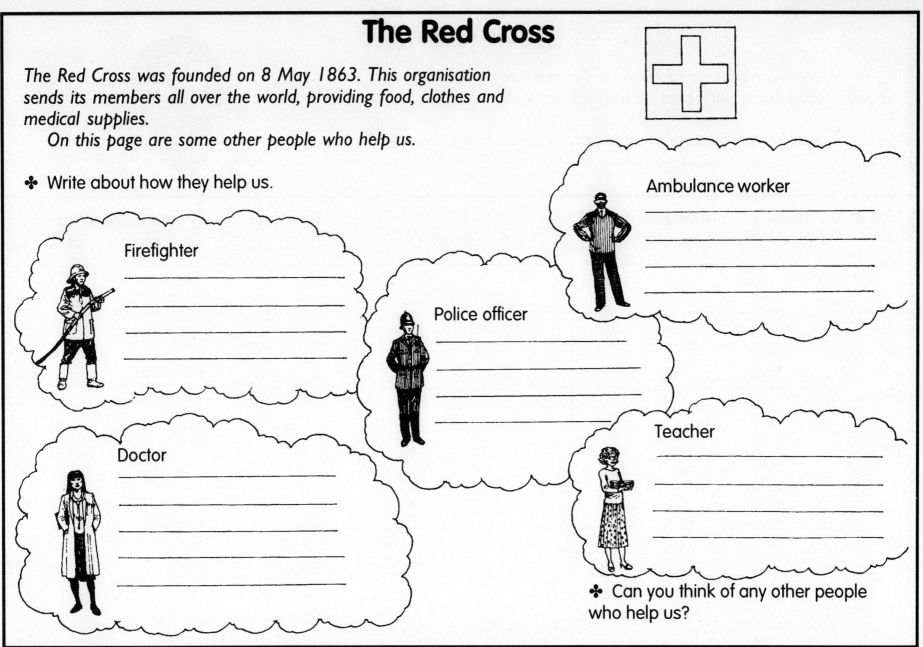

The Red Cross was founded on 8 May 1863. This organisation sends its members all over the world, providing food, clothes and medical supplies.

On this page are some other people who help us.

♣ Write about how they help us.

Ambulance worker
_____
_____
_____
_____

Firefighter
_____
_____
_____
_____

Police officer
_____
_____
_____
_____

Doctor
_____
_____
_____
_____

Teacher
_____
_____
_____

♣ Can you think of any other people who help us?

Name _____

Stevie Wonder

Stevie Wonder was born on 13 May 1950. He wrote his first hit song when he was 12 and since then he has had many more hits.

♣ Use this sheet to record your thoughts on different types of music.

Title of the piece	Instruments I could hear	Mood – things I thought of	Rhythm	Likes/dislikes – score out of 10

The Oscars

The first Academy awards, known as 'The Oscars', were presented on 16 May 1929. At this ceremony, awards called 'Oscars' are presented to people involved in making films.

♣ What are your favourite films?

♣ Design an 'Oscar' for someone in school who has done something special.

This Oscar is presented to _____
for _____ .

Name _____

Everest expedition

On 16 May 1975 Junko Tabei, from Japan, became the first woman to conquer Mount Everest.

❖ If you were to climb Mount Everest, what would you take with you and why? Think about: the weather, finding your way, communication links and food.

I would take:

❖ Write a letter to a friend telling them about your expedition and how you felt when you reached the summit of Mount Everest. Jot down some ideas here. Then draft your letter on the back of this page.

Helen Sharman

On 18 May 1991 Helen Sharman became Britain's first astronaut.

❖ Imagine an alien landed on our planet and asked you to help her find out about Earth. She needs to find examples of the things on this list. What would you suggest she looks for?

Something:	**Evidence of:**	**How do humans:**
• hard _____	• human beings _____	• travel?_____
• soft _____	_____	_____
• growing _____	• flying creatures _____	• stay alive? _____
• dead _____	_____	_____
• that helps plants to grow	• animals _____	• communicate?_____
_____	_____	_____
• to drink _____		• enjoy themselves?_____
• to eat _____		_____

Tomb treasures

Name _____

Tomb treasures

On 26 May 1954 archaeologists found the funeral ship of the Ancient Egyptian pharaoh Cheops near the Great Pyramid of Giza.

The Ancient Egyptians buried things with them which they thought would be of use in the Afterlife, such as furniture, food, clothes and riches.

♣ If you were going to have an afterlife, which things would you want to be buried with you and why?

I would want buried:

_____

_____

_____

_____

_____

_____

_____

June

1 _____	18 _____
2 _____	19 _____
3 _____	20 _____
4 _____	21 _____
5 _____	22 _____
6 _____	23 _____
7 _____	24 _____
8 _____	25 _____
9 _____	26 _____
10 _____	27 _____
11 _____	28 _____
12 _____	29 _____
13 _____	30 _____
14 _____	
15 _____	**Notes**
16 _____	
17 _____	**Birthdays**

Queen Elizabeth II

Name _____

Queen Elizabeth II

On 2 June 1953 Queen Elizabeth had her 'coronation'; the ceremony where she was publicly crowned queen.

♣ *Can you help? The Queen has lost her crown! Please design a new one for her.*

World Environment Day

5 June is World Environment Day. It was started by the United Nations to discuss caring for the world.

♣ With a group of friends, form a 'Green Team' for World Environment Day.

♣ Write an action plan for your team. What could you do to clean up your school grounds and classrooms and make them more environmentally friendly?

Think about: recycling, energy use, litter and so on.

♣ Design a badge for your team:

♣ What will be your team's motto?

_____

_____

Name _____

D-Day

During World War II, the German army occupied a large part of Europe. On 6 June 1944 troops from Britain, the United States of America, Canada and France invaded the beaches of Normandy in France in an attempt to end this German occupation. They were successful!

✤ Use an atlas to help you to answer these questions about Europe.

• What is the capital city of France?

• Which sea meets the shores of Spain, France, Italy and Greece?

• Which small country shares its borders with Belgium and France?

• Which famous mountain range borders northern Italy?

• In which countries are the following rivers:
  a Seine;   **b** Rhine;   **c** Thames?

• What is the capital city of Portugal?

• In which countries are the following cities:
  a Copenhagen;   **b** Athens;   **c** Edinburgh?

Charles Dickens

Charles Dickens died on 9 June 1870. He wrote many novels including A Christmas Carol *and* Oliver Twist.

In Dickens's story Oliver Twist, *Oliver is a little boy who lives in a workhouse. He longs for food...any food!*

♣ Imagine that you are Oliver dreaming about your favourite foods. Think of some more verses and finish our poem about food.

We love food, hot chocolate and mustard;
We love food, pepperoni, pizza and custard.

We love food,

The twenty pence coin

The twenty pence coin

The twenty pence coin was introduced into British money on 9 June 1982.

✤ How much is in each piggy bank?

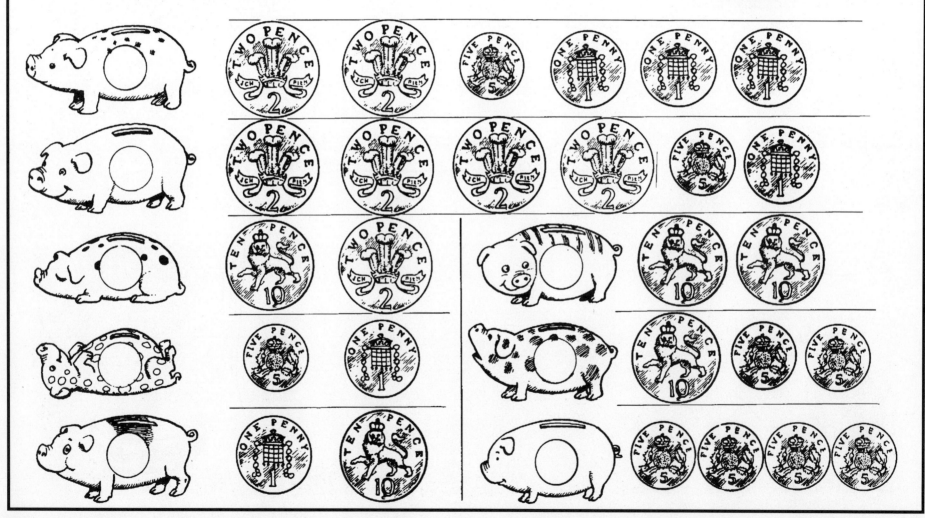

Wild things

Maurice Sendak was born on 10 June 1928. He is the author of several children's books including Where the Wild Things Are.

♣ Have a minibeast hunt around your school and look for some 'wild things'. Remember to be quiet and never hurt a living thing!

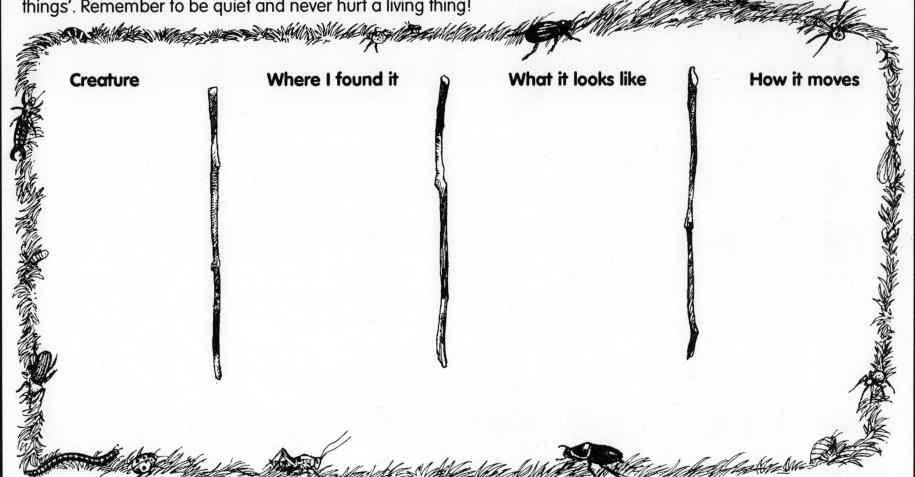

Creature	Where I found it	What it looks like	How it moves

Emmeline Pankhurst

Name _____

Emmeline Pankhurst

Emmeline Pankhurst was a 'suffragette'. She believed that women should be allowed to vote in political elections. Thanks to the suffragettes (founded in 1903), women were first allowed to vote in 1918, but only if they were over the age of 30!

Emmeline Pankhurst died on the 14 June 1928.

♣ Write a speech, using the evidence below, in support of the suffragettes.

What a Woman may be, and yet not have the Vote.				
Mayor	Nurse	Doctor	Mother	Factory Hand

What a Man may have been, and yet not lose the Vote.				

Convict	Lunatic	Unfit for Service	Proprietor of White Slaves	Drunk

_____

_____

_____

_____

_____

_____

_____

_____

_____

_____

_____

_____

_____

Name _____

The first woman in space

The first woman to travel in space was Valentina Tereshkova. Starting on the 16 June 1963 it took her 71 hours to travel around Earth 47 times.

♣ Use the words opposite to fill in the following statements about our Solar System. You may need reference books to help you.

• The Earth orbits the _____ once a year.

• The planet _____ is known as the 'red planet' because of its colour.

• _____ is the second largest planet and has rings made from ice.

• _____ is the planet closest to the Sun.

• _____ has fifteen moons.

• The smallest planet in our solar system is _____.

• The largest planet in our solar system is _____.

• _____ is the brightest planet when viewed from Earth.

• The _____ is not a planet, it is a star.

• _____ is the eighth planet.

♣ How many planets are there in our Solar System? ☐

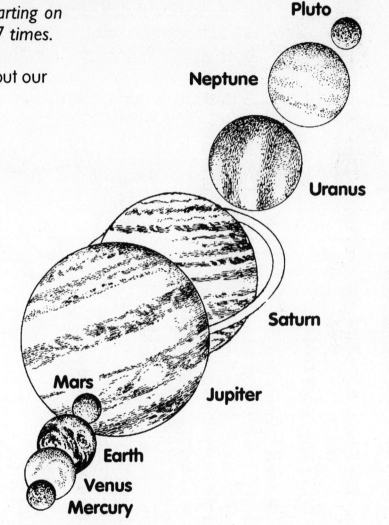

Pluto
Neptune
Uranus
Saturn
Jupiter
Mars
Earth
Venus
Mercury
Sun

Father's Day

Name _____

Father's Day

On the third Sunday in June we celebrate Father's Day.

✤ Make a Father's Day card.

You will need: scissors and coloured pencils or felt-tipped pens.
- Colour in this picture of the world and a dad. Can you make him look more like your dad?
- Cut out your picture and the stand. Don't forget to snip the slots.
- Write a message to your dad on the back of the picture.
- Now fit the slots in the picture into the slots in the stand. You will have to curve the picture round a bit. Your card will now stand up.

WORLD'S BEST DAD

Wimbledon

On 25 June 1969 the longest ever singles match was played at Wimbledon. It lasted 5 hours 12 minutes.

Sometimes, however, the tournament is affected by rain and play has to be stopped. The information below shows the rainfall during the first week's play at Wimbledon.

Day	1	2	3	4	5	6	7
Rainfall (mm)	5	1	0	4	2	9	0

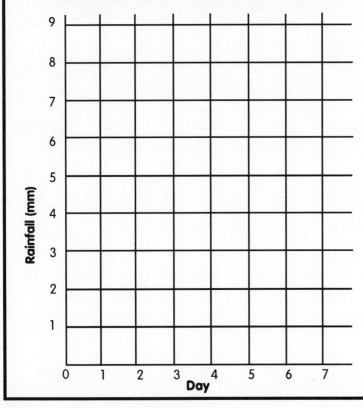

♣ Use the information opposite to draw the graph.

♣ Now use the graph to help you to answer these questions.

- Which day had the most rainfall? _____

- Which days had the least rainfall? _____

- On which days was play uninterrupted? _____

- On which day might play have been stopped by the rain? _____

- What was the range of rainfall over the seven days? _____

- What was the average amount of rainfall over the seven days? _____

♣ Design your own rain gauge and measure the rainfall each day for a week.

Name _____

July

1 _____
2 _____
3 _____
4 _____
5 _____
6 _____
7 _____
8 _____
9 _____
10 _____
11 _____
12 _____
13 _____
14 _____
15 _____
16 _____
17 _____

18 _____
19 _____
20 _____
21 _____
22 _____
23 _____
24 _____
25 _____
26 _____
27 _____
28 _____
29 _____
30 _____
31 _____

Notes
_____
_____

Birthdays
_____
_____
_____
_____

Name _____

Live Aid

On 13 July 1985 many famous rock music stars took part in a concert at Wembley Stadium, organised by Bob Geldof, to 'feed the world'. It was called 'Live Aid'. The money raised from the concert and records was sent to help famine victims in Africa.

♣ If a similar event were to happen today, which groups and artists would you want to take part?

♣ Design a CD cover to commemorate your concert.

Disneyland

Name _____

Disneyland

The 'Disneyland' theme park in California was opened on 18 July 1955.

❖ Can you help these people find their way around this theme park?

❖ Describe their routes. You could use the back of this page.

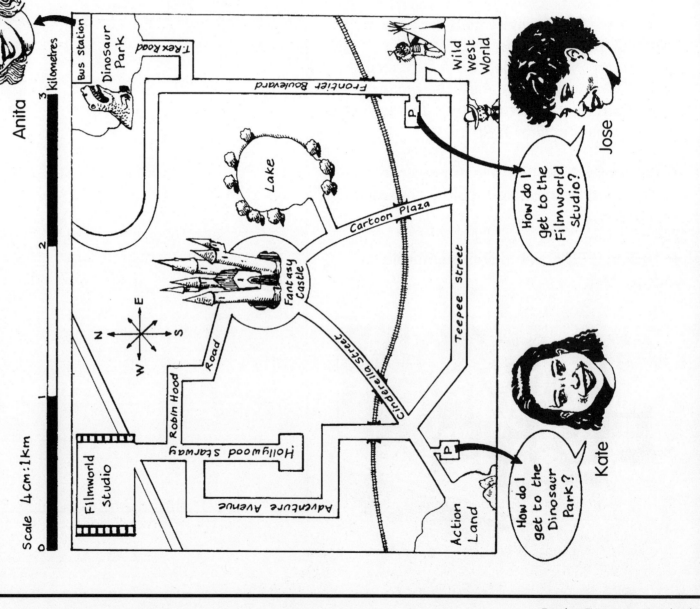

76

The first man on the Moon

On 21 July 1969, Neil Armstrong became the first man on the Moon. As he stepped on to the surface he said:

'That's one small step for a man, one giant leap for mankind.'

♣ What would be your first words to the people on Earth, if you were the first person to set foot on Mars?

_____
_____
_____
_____

♣ Draw a picture of the spacecraft which would take you to Mars.

♣ Who would you like to take with you? Draw them too.

Saint Christopher

Name _____

Saint Christopher

On 25 July Christians remember Saint Christopher, the patron saint of travellers.

♣ Carry out a 20 minute traffic survey near your school. You will need to find a safe place to stand and watch the passing vehicles.

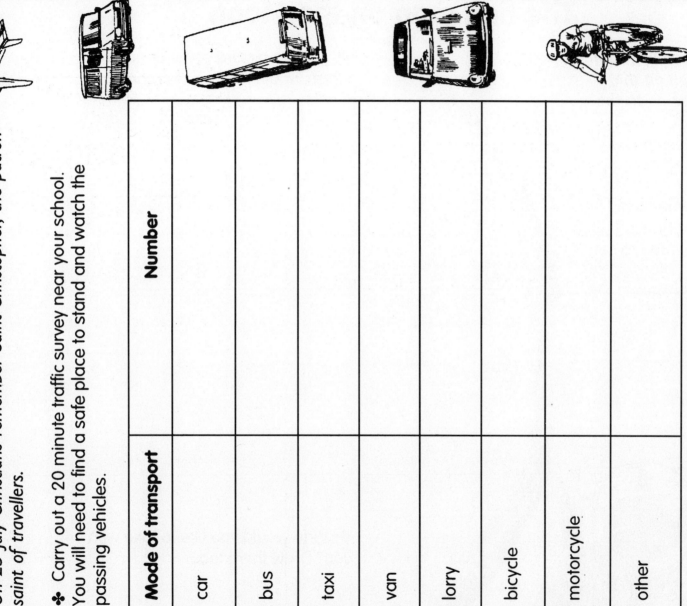

Mode of transport	Number
car	
bus	
taxi	
van	
lorry	
bicycle	
motorcycle	
other	

♣ Which is the most popular mode of transport?

♣ Which is the least popular mode of transport?

♣ Now carry out a survey to see how the children in your class travel to school.

Name _____

Henry Ford

Henry Ford, founder of the 'Ford Motor Company' who make Ford cars, was born on 30 July 1863.

♣ Look at the picture of a motor car opposite and others in brochures and magazines. Use them to help you to fill in the chart below listing the parts of a car, what they are made from and what they do.

Part	Materials	Function
wing mirrors	glass and metal and/or plastic	to see behind the car
tyre	rubber	to move the car

Robert Baden-Powell

Name _____

Robert Baden-Powell

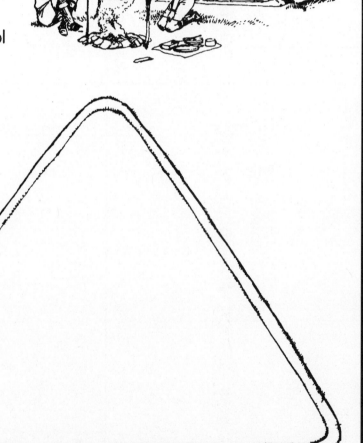

Robert Baden-Powell began the Scout Association around 31 July 1907. Today worldwide, girl and boy scouts promise always to do their best to serve God and the Queen and to try to help people every day. Scouts can take part in adventurous activities and can earn proficiency badges for things like first aid, sports and cookery.

♣ Design a Scout proficiency badge. You will need to choose a symbol for the activity it represents.

♣ How would the Scouts earn this badge?

_____

_____

_____

_____

_____

_____

Remember: 'Be prepared'.

Raksha bandhan

In July or August, Hindus celebrate Raksha bandhan, a festival in which girls tie 'rakhi' (twisted red and gold or yellow threads) around their brothers' wrists to protect them and strengthen the love between them.

♣ Not all brothers and sisters get on all the time. Imagine you have received this letter. How would you answer it?

Dear Friend,

Can you help me?

My sister and I do nothing but argue. We are always fighting over which television programme to watch. Last week, our Mum banned us from playing the computer game because we both wanted it at the same time. Also, my sister 'bugs' me because she wants to play football with me, and it's only for boys!

Yours sincerely,

Worried.

Dear Worried,

Summer holidays

Name _____

Summer holidays

✤ Use an atlas to help you to find out which country each of these places is in.

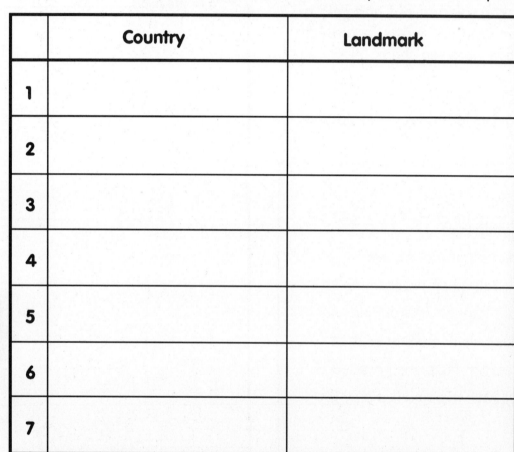

1 Cairo

2 Paris

3 Athens

4 New York

5 Sydney

6 Agra

7 London

	Country	Landmark
1		
2		
3		
4		
5		
6		
7		

✤ Now find out the names of each of these famous landmarks?

✤ Are you or any of your friends going on holiday – where are they going?

Here comes summer!

♣ Can you spot the differences between these two summer pictures? Circle them on the picture and then list them below.

Differences: _____

Flowers

Flowers

Throughout summer you will see a variety of flowers, but how closely do you really look?

♣ Use these words to label the parts of the flower opposite: style, ovule, petal, ovary, anther, stigma, filament.

♣ Match the part of the flower to its function to fill in these sentences.

• **A**_____ produce the yellow pollen which contains the male reproductive cells.

• The **o**_____ contain the female reproductive cells.

• **P**_____ attract insects. Sometimes they have nectaries attached to them containing nectar as food for the insects.

• The female reproductive cells which need to be fertilised by the pollen are called **o**_____ .

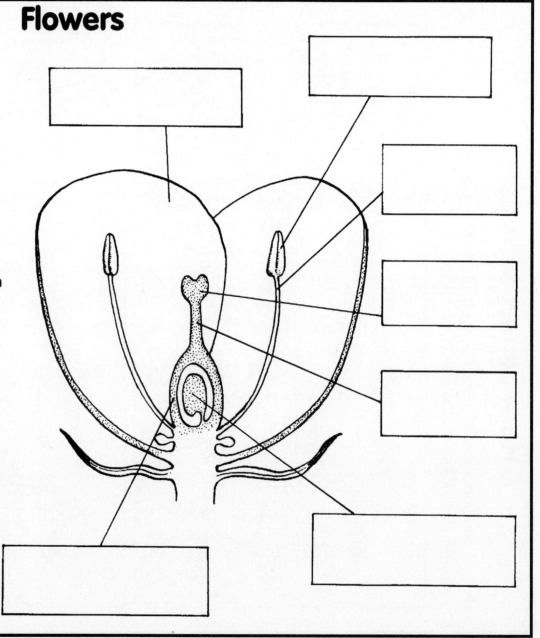

Name _____

August

1 _____	18 _____
2 _____	19 _____
3 _____	20 _____
4 _____	21 _____
5 _____	22 _____
6 _____	23 _____
7 _____	24 _____
8 _____	25 _____
9 _____	26 _____
10 _____	27 _____
11 _____	28 _____
12 _____	29 _____
13 _____	30 _____
14 _____	31 _____
15 _____	**Notes**
16 _____	
17 _____	**Birthdays**

Alexander Fleming

Alexander Fleming

Alexander Fleming was born on 6 August 1881. He was the scientist who discovered 'penicillin', an 'antibiotic', which kills bacteria in the body. Penicillin cures illnesses which were once incurable.

✤ Match the descriptions below to the correct organ.

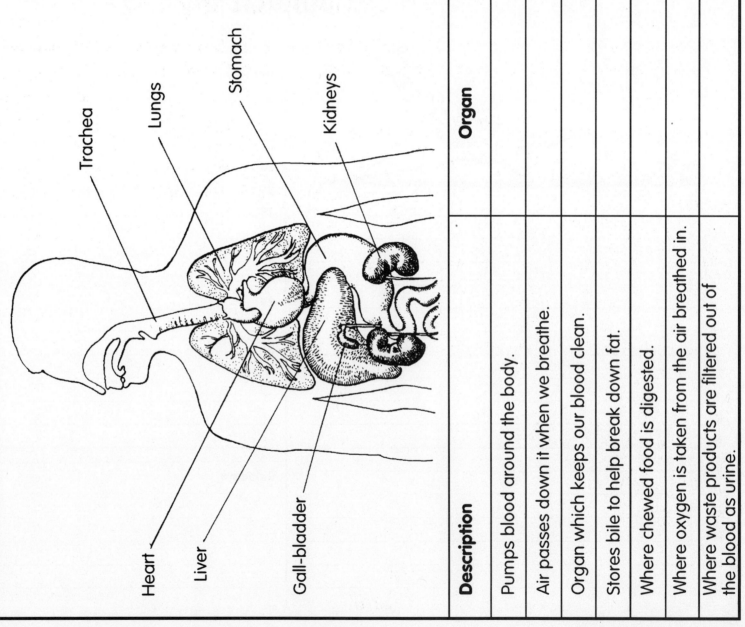

Trachea

Lungs

Stomach

Kidneys

Heart

Liver

Gall-bladder

Description	Organ					
Pumps blood around the body.						
Air passes down it when we breathe.						
Organ which keeps our blood clean.						
Stores bile to help break down fat.						
Where chewed food is digested.						
Where oxygen is taken from the air breathed in.						
Where waste products are filtered out of the blood as urine.						

John McCarthy

On 8 August 1991 John McCarthy was freed by his captors after spending five years as a hostage in the Lebanon.

♣ Imagine if you had been kept as a hostage for this long. How do you think you might be feeling and what things would you miss?

♣ Draw a picture of the one place you would miss the most.

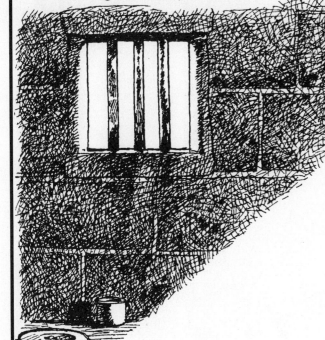

Alfred Hitchcock

Alfred Hitchcock was a famous film director who was born on 13 August 1899. His films were usually 'thrillers'.

♣ Can you write a thrilling story? Continue on the back of this sheet if you need more room.

'Oh no! Not another spelling test,' said Johnny Begood, who was having his usual Monday morning moan.
    At first glance, Strictville Primary School seemed just like any other school. However, the recent stock room disappearances were beginning to cause concern...

STOCK ROOM

The Tay Bridge

On 18 August 1906 one of Britain's longest road bridges, the Tay Bridge, was officially opened.

♣ Imagine that a new road bridge is to be built near your town, Sleepy Hollows. The road from the bridge will cut across Farmer Turnip's farm. However, this will make the journey from Sleepy Hollows to the nearby motorway much quicker.

♣ What do you think each of these people would say about the new road and bridge?

Mr I M Green, a local resident who is concerned about the environment:

Farmer Turnip:

Mr J Ceebee, a road builder who will need 30 people to build the road:

Mrs B Quicker, who uses the motorway to get to work:

Martin Luther King, jun.

Martin Luther King, jun.

Martin Luther King, jun. was a young Baptist minister from Alabama (USA). He spoke out against racism.

On 28 August 1963 he told a crowd of 200,000 people in Washington, 'I have a dream.'

♣ What was his dream about? Find out and write about it below.

♣ What would your dream be to make the world a better place?

I have a dream...

Name _____

Vacuum cleaner

On 30 August 1901 Hubert Cecil Booth completed his invention — the first successful vacuum cleaner.

♣ Imagine you are an inventor and have designed something which dusts or washes up or makes beds.

♣ Draw it here:

♣ Use the space below to tell everyone what it is made from, how it is powered and why it is brilliant!

Name of invention:

_____

Diary page: September

September

18 _____
19 _____
20 _____
21 _____
22 _____
23 _____
24 _____
25 _____
26 _____
27 _____
28 _____
29 _____
30 _____

1 _____
2 _____
3 _____
4 _____
5 _____
6 _____
7 _____
8 _____
9 _____
10 _____
11 _____
12 _____
13 _____
14 _____
15 _____
16 _____
17 _____

Notes

_____
_____
_____

Birthdays

_____
_____
_____
_____

The Great Fire of London

The Great Fire of London started on Sunday 2 September 1666 in a baker's shop on Pudding Lane. Over 100,000 people were left homeless because of the fire. It is unlikely that such an event would happen today because of the different materials used in building and the improved technology used by fire-fighters.

✤ Look at the two pictures below. They show people fighting the Great Fire of London and modern fire-fighting equipment.

✤ Describe how fire-fighting has changed since the Great Fire of London.

Then

Now

The first library

The first library

The first public library in Britain was opened in Manchester on 6 September 1852.

❧ Write a set of dos and don'ts for someone using a library for the first time.

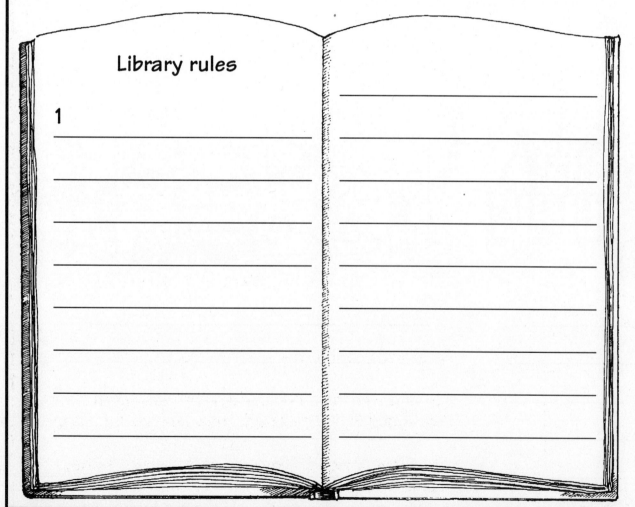

Library rules

1

❧ What is the difference between fiction and non-fiction?

The first SOS broadcast

On 10 September 1923 the first SOS message (Save Our Souls) was broadcast on radio by the BBC using Morse code. Morse code messages can be transmitted by sound, using long and short sounds, or by light, using long and short flashes. Morse code is written as a pattern of dots and dashes.

♣ To send a message to a friend using Morse code, set up an electrical circuit with a bulb, like this:

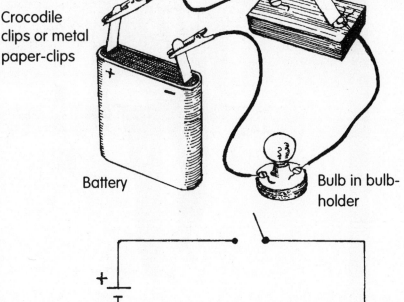

Crocodile clips or metal paper-clips

Commercial switch or metal paper-clips

Battery

Bulb in bulb-holder

This is the Morse code:

A • —   B — •••   C — • — •   D — • •

E •   F •• — •   G — — •   H ••••

I ••   J • — — —   K — • —   L • — ••

M — —   N — •   O — — —   P • — — •

Q — — • —   R • — •   S •••   T —

U •• —   V ••• —   W • — —   X — •• —

Y — • — —   Z — — ••

In Morse code: ••• / — — — / ••• means SOS.

♣ Agree on the amount of time between each letter (for example, five seconds). Then send your message.

♣ Ask your friend to write down the letters as they come through.

Name _____

Jesse Owens

Jesse Owens was a black American athlete who was born on 12 September 1913. He set 11 world records in track and field events and at the 1936 Olympic games in Germany won four gold medals.

♣ Imagine you had been asked to interview him. What questions would you have asked?

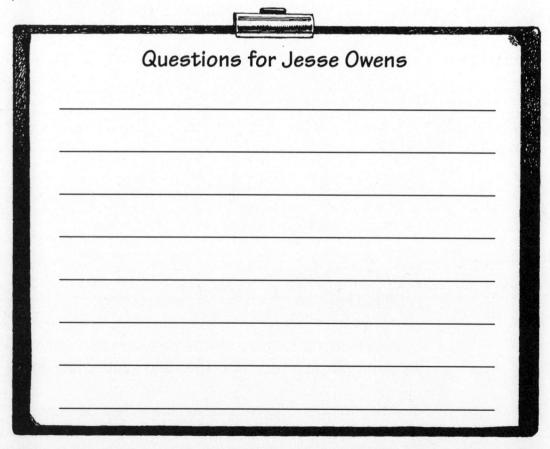

Questions for Jesse Owens

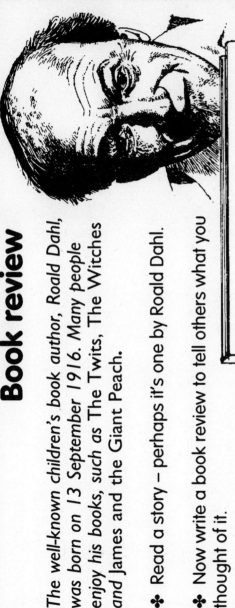

Book review

The well-known children's book author, Roald Dahl, was born on 13 September 1916. Many people enjoy his books, such as The Twits, The Witches and James and the Giant Peach.

♣ Read a story – perhaps it's one by Roald Dahl.

♣ Now write a book review to tell others what you thought of it.

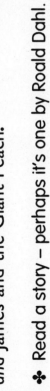

● The title of my book was: _____

● The author of my book was: _____

● My book was about: _____

● My favourite part of the book was: _____
because: _____

● At the end of the book: _____

● Here are three words that describe the book I read: _____

● I would give this book [   ] out of 10.

Agatha Christie

Agatha Christie

Agatha Christie was born on 15 September 1890. She was famous for her mystery stories. Her 'ace investigator' was called Hercule Poirot.

♣ Imagine you have started your own private detective agency. Lady Upstart's diamonds have been stolen. Write to tell her why you are an 'ace investigator' and should handle the case.

Private **DETECTIVE** Agency

Dear Lady Upstart,

Yours sincerely,

Ace investigator

♣ Can you think of any other famous investigators, detectives or secret agents?

Autumn leaves

The season of autumn begins around 22 September.

♣ How many leaves are there on each tree?

♣ How many leaves are there on the ground under each tree?

The marathon

Name _____

The marathon

On 29 September 490 BC a Greek soldier called Pheidippides ran from Marathon to Athens, a distance of 26 miles 385 yards (42km 195m), to deliver the news of a Greek victory in a battle. A race of this distance was first included in the modern Olympic games in 1896 and named after Marathon, in Greece, where that battle and the famous run took place.

♣ Below are the times it took ten runners to complete a marathon. If the race started at 15:00, work out each runner's finishing time and position.

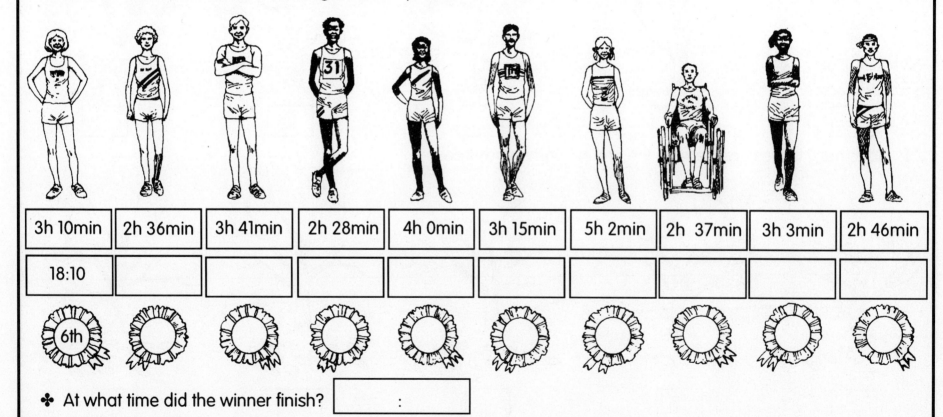

3h 10min	2h 36min	3h 41min	2h 28min	4h 0min	3h 15min	5h 2min	2h 37min	3h 3min	2h 46min
18:10									
6th									

♣ At what time did the winner finish? [:]

Back to school

At the beginning of September many children return to school after the long summer holidays.

♣ If you could design your own school uniform, what would it look like? What colours would you use? Sketch your designs on to these two models.

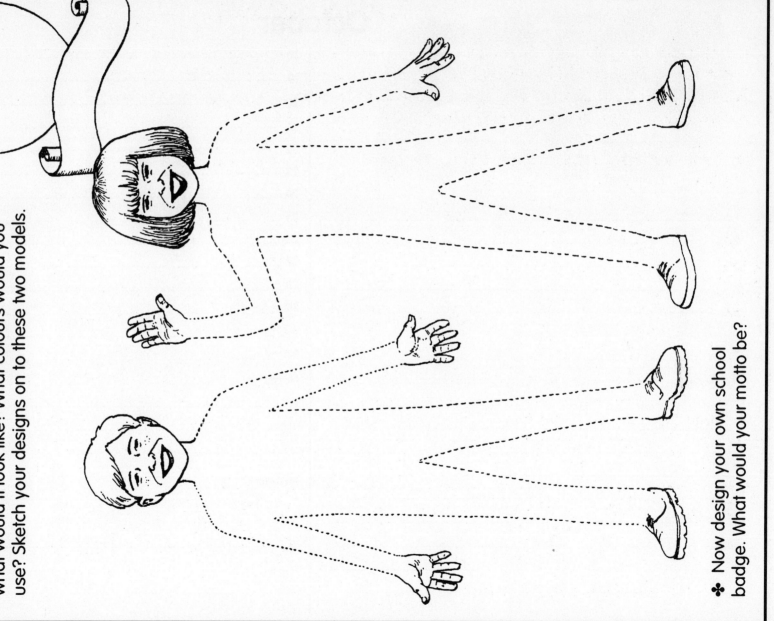

♣ Now design your own school badge. What would your motto be?

Diary page: October

Name _____

October

1 _____
2 _____
3 _____
4 _____
5 _____
6 _____
7 _____
8 _____
9 _____
10 _____
11 _____
12 _____
13 _____
14 _____
15 _____
16 _____
17 _____

18 _____
19 _____
20 _____
21 _____
22 _____
23 _____
24 _____
25 _____
26 _____
27 _____
28 _____
29 _____
30 _____
31 _____

Notes

_____

_____

Birthdays

_____

_____

The first postcard

The first ever postcard was issued in Austria on 1 October 1869.

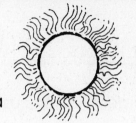

✤ Imagine you are away on holiday. Write this postcard to send home to a friend. Tell them all about your holiday.

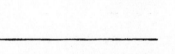

_____

_____

_____

_____

_____

♣ Now turn over and draw the picture for the postcard showing your holiday destination.

Name _____

Fast food

On 1 October 1974 McDonald's opened their first British restaurant in London.

❖ Devise your own burger meal and use the menu below to describe what is in it.

❖ Draw your burger in the bun below.

Menu

All for only £ _____

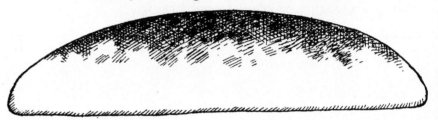

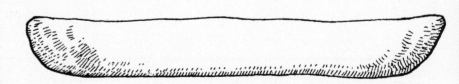

❖ Do some market research to find out which fast food meal is the most popular in your class.

Hairstyles

On 8 October 1906 Karl Nessler invented a new wavy hairstyle called the 'perm'.

♣ Design some new hairstyles of your own using the models opposite. Give each of your styles a name.

♣ Collect some data about the hairstyles (for example, long, short, curly, straight and so on) and hair colours in your class.

♣ Present your data using a graph.

The mattress style

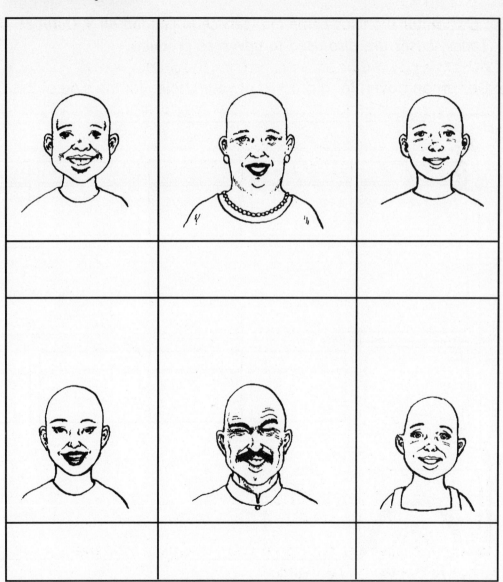

The first motor omnibus

The first motor omnibus

The first motor omnibus came into service in London on 9 October 1906.
    Today, buses are also used to advertise products.

✤ Design an advert for a product of your choice for the side of this London double decker.

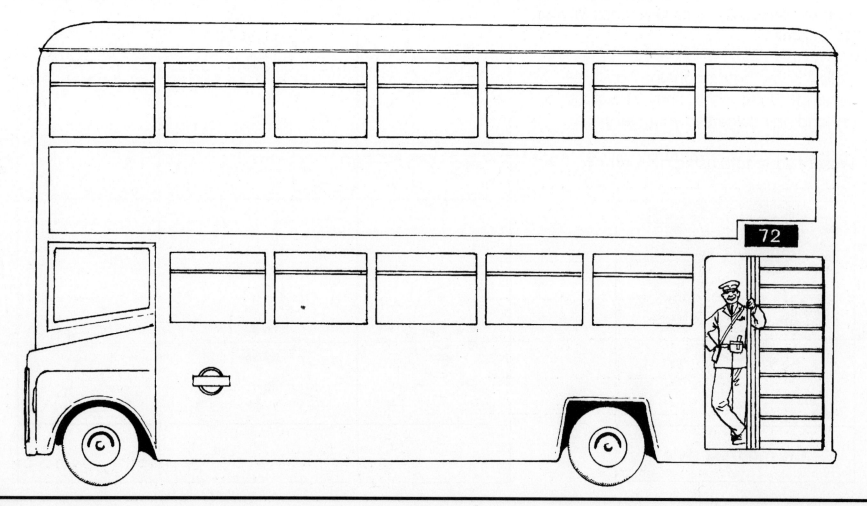

Potato crisps

Square-shaped crisps became so popular that on 12 October 1981 'Smiths' bought extra land in Lincolnshire so that more potatoes could be grown.

♣ Find out which is the most popular flavour of crisps in your class. Record your findings using a bar graph.

♣ Think of a new flavour of crisps that might be popular – 'sardine and egg flavour', perhaps.

♣ Now design a new style bag for your crisps.

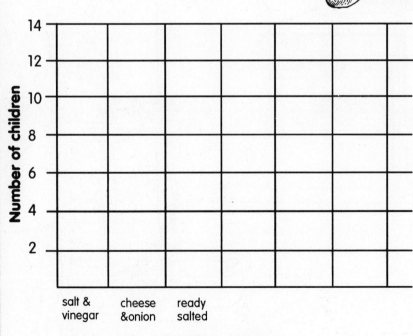

Name _____

Electricity

On 19 October 1751 Benjamin Franklin discovered that lightning was electricity. He was flying his kite during a thunderstorm, when a bolt of lightning hit the kite and produced a spark.

❖ How many things can you spot in this picture that use electricity?

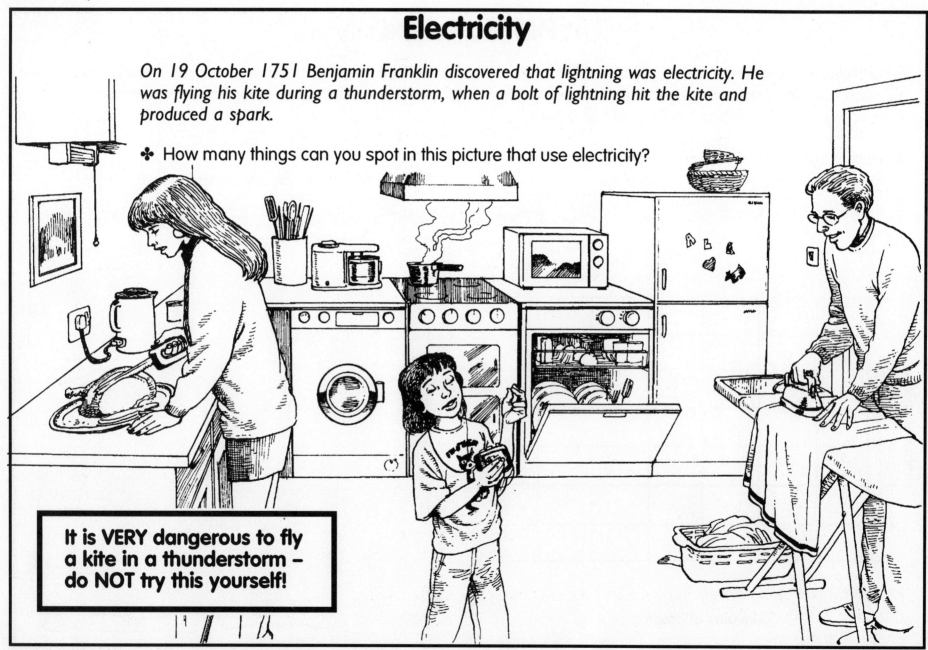

It is VERY dangerous to fly a kite in a thunderstorm – do NOT try this yourself!

United Nations Day

24 October is United Nations Day and is celebrated in almost every country in the world in the hope of preventing another world war.

♣ Design a United Nations flag which shows the message of the world's people working together for peace.

Hallowe'en

Hallowe'en

31 October is Hallowe'en; the eve of All Saints' Day. Hallowe'en is made up of two words: 'hallow' meaning 'saintly' and 'e'en' meaning 'evening'. It is the night when witches, fairies and goblins are said to hold their annual celebrations with dancing and mischief. Traditionally, people dress up as ghosts or witches and have Hallowe'en parties.

♣ Write a description of what you can see in this spooky Hallowe'en scene.

♣ Can you write a ghost story?

Name _____

Harvest festival

During autumn, farmers gather in their fully-grown crops. This is called 'harvesting'. Believers of many religions give thanks to their god for the harvest.

✤ Cut out the pictures below and stick them on to another sheet of paper in the correct order.

✤ Write about what is happening in each picture.

Name _____

Autumn apple appetisers

Autumn apple appetisers

♣ Do some baking for yourself and a friend. Get an adult to help you follow these instructions to make 'Autumn apple appetisers'.

You will need:

2 large cooking apples

syrup or brown sugar

sultanas or currants

a little butter or margarine for greasing tray

cream or ready-made custard (optional)

an apple-corer

a baking tray

a dessertspoon

greaseproof paper

1 Grease the baking tray with a little butter or margarine on a piece of greaseproof paper.

2 Wash each apple and carefully take out the core using the apple-corer.

3 Place the apples on the greased baking tray.

4 Fill the apples with a dessertspoonful of syrup or brown sugar and a few sultanas or currants.

5 Bake the apples at 180°C/Gas Mark 4 for about 25 minutes.

6 Serve the apples on their own or with the custard or cream.

7 Enjoy your 'Autumn apple appetisers'!

Name _____

November

1 _____
2 _____
3 _____
4 _____
5 _____
6 _____
7 _____
8 _____
9 _____
10 _____
11 _____
12 _____
13 _____
14 _____
15 _____
16 _____
17 _____

18 _____
19 _____
20 _____
21 _____
22 _____
23 _____
24 _____
25 _____
26 _____
27 _____
28 _____
29 _____
30 _____

Notes
_____
_____
_____

Birthdays
_____
_____
_____
_____

Name _____

All Saints' Day

On 1 November Christians celebrate All Saints' Day. Saints are special people known for their holiness and their good deeds. Roman Catholic Christians believe that St Veronica did a good deed for Jesus while he was alive.

♣ Cut out the pictures below and put them in the correct order to tell the story of Saint Veronica.

Then Veronica came. She was scared, but she wanted to help Jesus, so she pushed past the soldiers.

Veronica left and went home.

Veronica took off her veil and used it to wipe Jesus' face.

Jesus thanked Veronica with a smile.

Jesus was carrying the cross. He fell, but no one helped him. All around people were laughing and shouting at him.

At home, Veronica looked at her veil and saw the face of Jesus on it.

Bonfire Night

❖ Brainstorm about things that you can see, smell, feel, taste and hear on Bonfire Night (5 November).

❖ Use these ideas to complete this poem.

Bonfire Night is

Seeing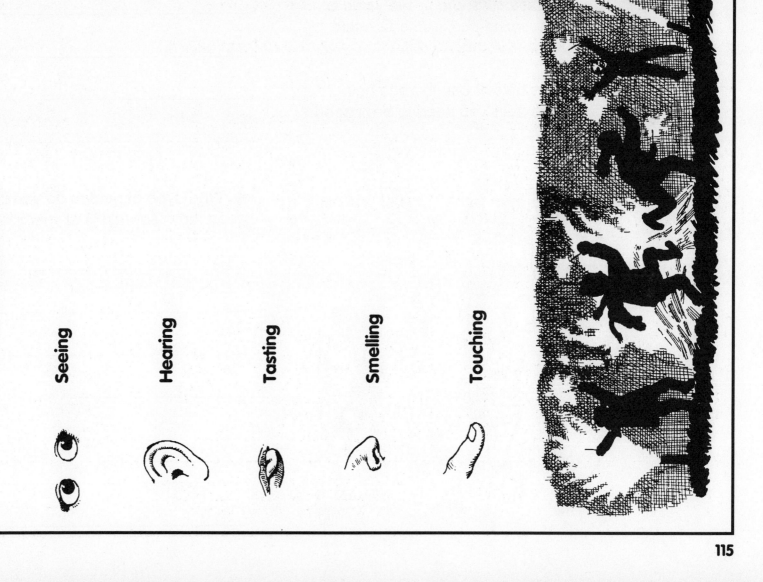

Hearing

Tasting

Smelling

Touching

Basketball

Name _____

Basketball

James Naismith, a Canadian, was born on 6 November 1861. He originated the game of basketball in 1891. Basketball is one of the world's most popular sports, becoming part of the Olympic games in 1936.

♣ Look at the drawings below. Use them to help you to make a list of the skills you need to be a good basketball player.

The skills needed are:_____

_____

_____

_____

_____

♣ What type of person do you think would make a good team captain? List your ideas below.

_____

_____

_____

_____

_____

_____

_____

_____

Buried treasure

Robert Louis Stevenson, the author, was born in Edinburgh on 13 November 1850. One of his most famous books is Treasure Island *about the adventures of Jim Hawkins and Long John Silver.*

✤ Find each of the objects on Long John Silver's list on the map. Write the coordinates of each object on to the list.

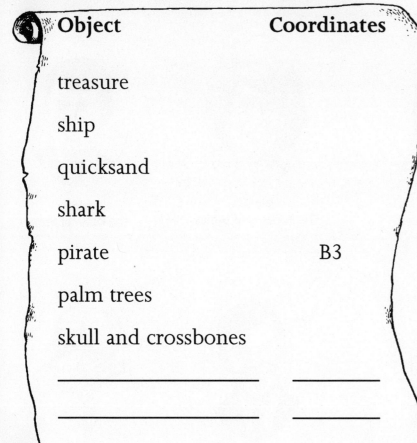

Object	Coordinates
treasure	
ship	
quicksand	
shark	
pirate	B3
palm trees	
skull and crossbones	
_____	_____
_____	_____

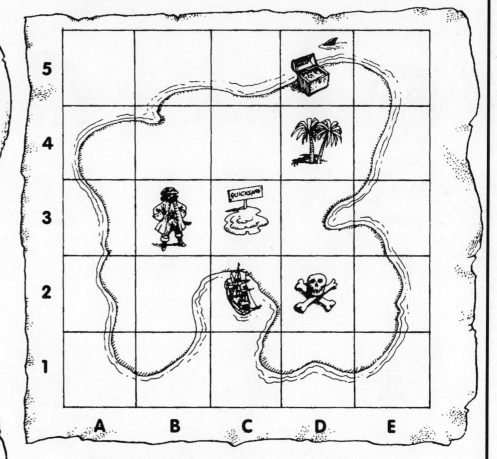

✤ Add some objects of your own to Long John Silver's list and to the map.

Name _____

Family trees

*Charles, The Prince of Wales, was born on 14 November 1948.
The drawings below show members of Charles's family.*

♣ Cut out these pictures and make a royal family tree.

**Charles
The Prince of Wales**

**Queen Elizabeth
The Queen Mother**

**Elizabeth II
Her Majesty The Queen**

**Diana
The Princess of Wales**

**Andrew
The Duke of York**

Prince William

**Prince Henry
(Harry)**

**Prince Philip
The Duke of Edinburgh**

Prince Edward

**Anne
The Princess Royal**

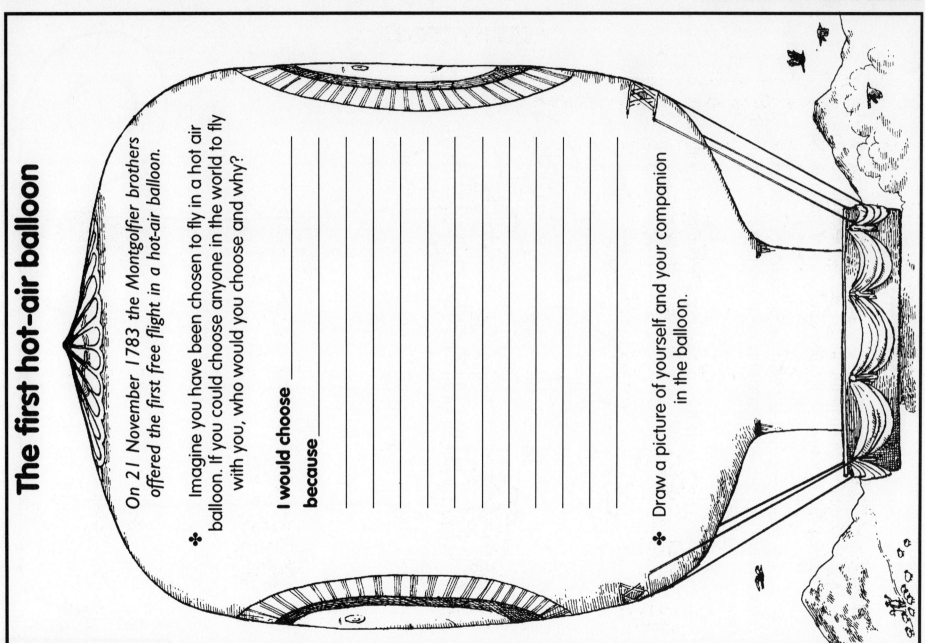

The first hot-air balloon

On 21 November 1783 the Montgolfier brothers offered the first free flight in a hot-air balloon.

♣ Imagine you have been chosen to fly in a hot air balloon. If you could choose anyone in the world to fly with you, who would you choose and why?

I would choose _____

because _____

♣ Draw a picture of yourself and your companion in the balloon.

Name _____

Diwali

Diwali

Diwali is a Hindu celebration in honour of the goddess Lakshmi, who is the guardian of wealth and prosperity. People welcome her into their homes with paintings on the floor and rows of lamps or candles.

♣ Write a shape poem about light. Some words are already in place to get you started. Brainstorm some more words and ideas concerning light.

♣ Write your words on to the candle shape to complete your poem.

fiery

illuminating

Feed the birds

It can be difficult for birds to survive a harsh winter.

♣ Why not make a winter bird-cake?

You will need to collect:

125g lard
some or all of the following
– brown breadcrumbs,
currants, bacon rind,
chopped apple, peanuts
(not salted), stale cake or
biscuits
a saucepan
a large bowl
a dessertspoon
empty yoghurt or mousse
pots
2 pieces of string, each
about 40cm long
scissors

1 Make a hole in the bottom of each yoghurt pot. Make a knot in one end of each piece of string and thread one string through the hole in each pot, so that the knots are inside them.

2 Melt the lard in the saucepan.

3 Put all the other ingredients in the bowl and pour in the melted lard.

4 Stir the mixture well and spoon it into the pots. Press the mixture down firmly.

5 Leave the bird-cakes to set. Then remove the pots carefully and hang up the cakes for the birds.

Bird-watcher's diary

Bird-watcher's diary

Bird-watchers often go to remote places and travel long distances to watch rare birds.

♣ Use this chart to record the birds that come to your school grounds. Put your own choice of bird in the last box.

Name of bird	Date	How many?	Name of bird	Date	How many?
jay			blue-tit		
chaffinch			song thrush		
starling			blackbird		
robin			_____		

Name _____

December

1 _____	18 _____
2 _____	19 _____
3 _____	20 _____
4 _____	21 _____
5 _____	22 _____
6 _____	23 _____
7 _____	24 _____
8 _____	25 _____
9 _____	26 _____
10 _____	27 _____
11 _____	28 _____
12 _____	29 _____
13 _____	30 _____
14 _____	31 _____
15 _____	**Notes**
16 _____	
17 _____	**Birthdays**

Walt Disney

Name _____

Walt Disney

Walt Disney was born on 3 December 1901. He created many lovable cartoon characters including Mickey Mouse, Donald Duck and Goofy.

♣ Can you create a cartoon character? Fill in the details below. Then draw your character in the frame opposite.

Name _____

How does he or she behave? _____

_____

_____

What antics does she or he get up to?

_____

_____

_____

What is the character's 'catch phrase'?

_____

The first heart transplant

The first heart transplant was performed on 3 December 1967. Few people ever need a heart transplant, and we can help to keep our hearts healthy by eating a balanced diet and exercising regularly.

Are you fit?

♣ Take your pulse for 15 seconds. Multiply it by 4 to work out what your resting pulse is per minute.

My resting pulse rate is _____ .

♣ With an adult present, do some non-stop step-ups on to a bench for _____ minutes.

♣ Immediately afterwards take your pulse again and record it. Then record your pulse every 2 minutes.

Time after exercise	Pulse rate
Straight after	
2 mins after	
4 mins after	
6 mins after	

The quicker your pulse returns to its resting rate the fitter you are likely to be.

The first motorway

On 5 December 1958 Harold Macmillan officially opened Britain's first stretch of motorway.

✤ List some of the advantages and disadvantages of motorways.

Think about:

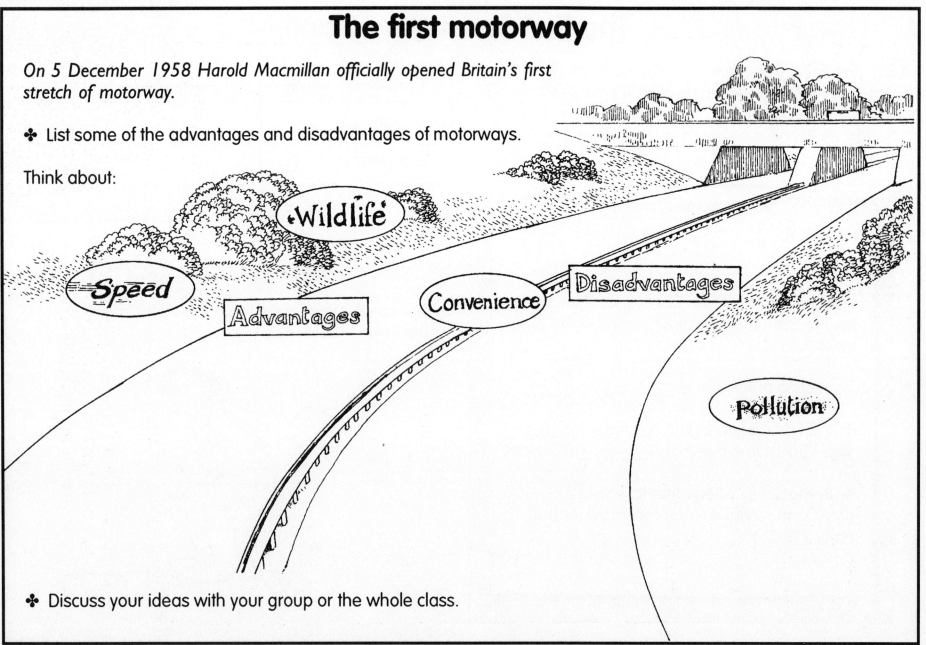

✤ Discuss your ideas with your group or the whole class.

Name _____

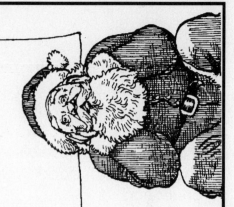

Saint Nicholas

Saint Nicholas's feast day is 6 December. Saint Nicholas is the patron saint of children. He is also known as 'Santa Claus'. Just before Christmas many children write to Santa Claus to tell him what they have been doing and what they would like for Christmas.

♣ Write a letter to Santa.

Dear Santa,

♣ Santa Claus is sad. Can you cheer him up by drawing a present for him that would be really useful? You could use the back of this page.

Name _____

Big Ben

On 11 December 1981 the mechanism inside Big Ben froze and the clock came to a halt between 12.27 pm and 1.30 pm.

♣ These clocks have also stopped. What time is shown on each clock? Write the digital clock time under each one.

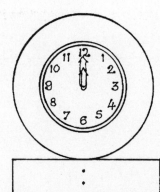

♣ Make a list of all the things that you think might happen if all the clocks in the world stopped at the same time!

We'd all be late for school.

The dinners would get burned.

_____

_____

_____

_____

_____

_____

_____

_____

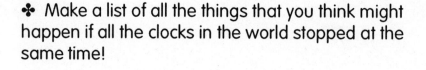

Beethoven

On 16 December 1770 the German composer, Ludwig van Beethoven, was born in Bonn in Germany.

♣ Can you compose your own music? Make some instruments using everyday objects.

Here are some ideas:

Tap or blow over bottles.

Hanging objects make good chimes.

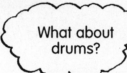

What about drums?

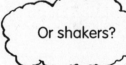

Or shakers?

♣ Can you think of any more ideas?

♣ What will you need to make your instruments?

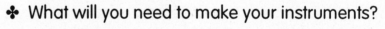

_____

_____

_____

♣ Now perform your music for the class.

The Christmas story

The Christmas story

25 December is Christmas Day. This is the day when Christians celebrate the birth of Jesus.

♣ Below is the Christmas story, but some of the words are missing! Can you fill in the missing words?

The angel _____ appeared to Mary to tell her that her baby was to be called

_____ . Mary and _____ rode on a donkey into _____ to register in

the Roman census. When they got to the _____ there was no room, but the innkeeper

offered them the _____ which _____ and Joseph accepted. Baby Jesus slept in

a _____ . Meanwhile an _____ appeared to some _____ who were

tending their sheep on the hillside, to tell them the good news about Jesus' birth. Then the

_____ _____ followed a _____ to the stable. There

the three kings offered gifts of _____ , _____ and_____ .

shepherds   stable   myrrh   inn   three kings   Mary   gold   manger
frankincense   angel   Bethlehem   Jesus   Gabriel   star   Joseph

Hanukkah

Hanukkah, the Jewish 'Festival of Lights', is celebrated over eight days in December. During the festival a menorah (or candlestick) is placed in the window of Jewish homes as a sign of God's presence. The menorah holds nine candles which are lit, one more each night, during the festival. The middle candle is a 'servant' used for lighting the others.

♣ Create a design for this menorah.

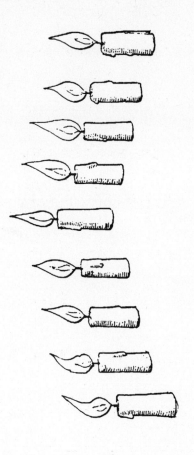

Hijra

Name _____

Hijra

Hijra is a Muslim new year festival when Muslims remember how their prophet, Muhammad, went from Mecca to Medina and there built the first mosque.

♣ Imagine that you have been given the job of finding a place to build a new town. What things would you include in your new town? How would you try to make it a friendly community?

♣ Give your new town a name and then list your proposals (ideas) below.

My proposals for: _____

(town's name)

All about me

♣ Record information about yourself on this form.

Name: _____

Hobbies/interests: _____

_____

Favourite food: _____

Favourite TV programme: _____

Favourite games: _____

People I admire: _____

My aims for this year

In school I want to improve: _____

_____

At home I want to improve: _____

_____

What I would like to be doing in 20 years time: _____

_____

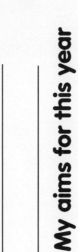

All about my work

All about my work

♣ On this form record information about topics you have covered, activities you have enjoyed or exciting new facts you have learned during the year.

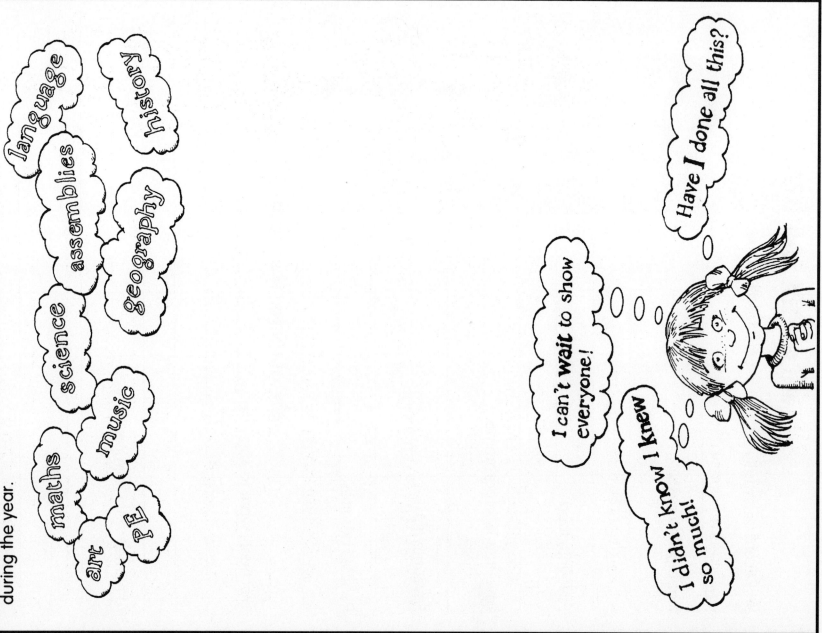

Name _____

All about my holiday

♣ Fill in this form to tell us all about your holiday.

● Things my family and I did:
_____
_____

● My favourite place we visited:
_____

● Things I enjoyed doing the most:
_____

● What I did with my friends:
_____

● My favourite holiday TV programme:
_____

● The toy I played with the most:
_____

● The funniest thing that happened:
_____

● New things that I did:
_____
_____

Year round quiz

Name _____

Year round quiz

❧ Which is the first month of the year?

_____

❧ Which month comes after March?

_____

❧ Which month comes before June?

_____

❧ Which month comes after August, but before October?

_____

❧ How many months are there in a year?

_____

❧ In which month is:

• your birthday? _____

• Christmas Day? _____

• Bonfire Night? _____

• April Fool's Day? _____

January
February
March
April
May
June
July
August
September
October
November
December

❧ To which season might each of these words belong? Write them in the correct box on the diagram.

Autumn	Winter
Spring	Summer

Weather headlines

✤ Write two newspaper reports using the headlines below. Jot some ideas on the back of this sheet. Think about the effect of the weather on peoples' lives! Why not include interviews and experts' comments?

THE POST

Britain sizzles as drought continues

The NEWS

All Washed Up
Floods hit North Wales

Weather watch

These two pictures show the same garden in summer and in winter.

♣ Which picture is which? What differences can you see?

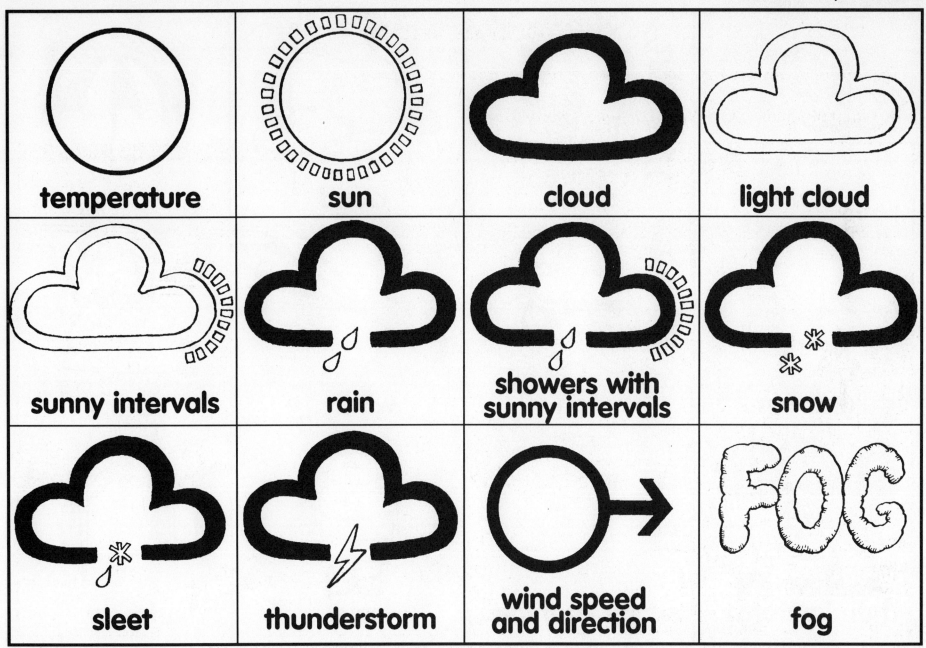

temperature

sun

cloud

light cloud

sunny intervals

rain

showers with
sunny intervals

snow

sleet

thunderstorm

wind speed
and direction

fog

Weather symbols: 2

hot	sunny	cloud	rain
light rain	fog	windy	snow
thunderstorm	sunny intervals	cold	frosty

Summer

Name _____

Name _____

Winter